THE THEORY OF SOUND IN ITS RELATION TO MUSIC

THE THEORY OF SOUND IN ITS RELATION TO MUSIC.

BY

PROFESSOR PIETRO BLASERNA

GYAN

Published by

Gyan Publishing House
5, Ansari Road
Daryaganj, New Delhi-110002
Phone: 011-47034999, 9811692060
E-mail: books@gyanbooks.com

Distribution Network
gyanbooks.com
India, USA, Canada, UK, Australia

ISBN: 978-93-6280-338-2 (PB)
First Published, 1876

2nd Impression 2024

Printed at: Gyan Press, Delhi.

THE THEORY OF SOUND IN ITS RELATION TO MUSIC
Author: PIETRO BLASERNA

THE

INTERNATIONAL SCIENTIFIC SERIES.

NOTE TO THE ENGLISH EDITION.

A FEW of the woodcuts in this work were designed by Professor TYNDALL for his book on Sound. They are here reproduced by his kind permission.

THE THEORY OF SOUND IN ITS RELATION TO MUSIC.

BY

PROFESSOR PIETRO BLASERNA,

OF THE ROYAL UNIVERSITY OF ROME.

WITH NUMEROUS WOODCUTS.

1876.

PREFACE.

The present treatise neither pretends to nor aims at giving a complete description or demonstration of the phenomena of Sound, or of the history and laws of Music. Those who wish to study these subjects thoroughly, whether from their scientific or artistic aspect, must have recourse to special works and special study.

Following the example given by Helmholtz in his now classical book, "Die Lehre von den Tonempfindungen," I have tried to bring together in a plain and simple form two subjects which have hitherto been treated of separately. The student of physics did not go much into the study of musical arguments, and our artists do not sufficiently understand the very important bearing that the laws of sound have upon many musical questions.

Science has latterly made notable progress in this respect. She has come to regard the history of the development of Music from a single point of view, and is on the road to furnish a larger and firmer basis to musical criticism.

To expound briefly the fundamental principles of such a science, and to point out its most important applications, has been the object and scope of this treatise. I hope, therefore, that it will be received with some interest both by lovers of science and by lovers of art.

PIETRO BLASERNA.

April 1875.

CONTENTS.

CHAPTER I.

PAGE

1. Periodic movements, vibration—2. Sonorous vibration.—3. Vibration of a bell—4. Vibration of a tuning-fork, graphic method—5. Vibration of a string—6. Of plates and membranes—7. Vibration of air in a sounding pipe—8. Method by the manometric flame—9. Conclusion . . . 1

CHAPTER II.

1. Transmission of sound—2. Propagation in air—3. In water and other bodies—4. Velocity of sound in air—5. In water and other bodies—6. Reflection of sound—7. Echo . 28

CHAPTER III.

1. Characteristics of sound, and difference between musical sound and noise—2. Loudness of sound, and the various causes on which it depends—3. Principle of the superposition of sounds—4. Sounding-boards and resonators . 45

CHAPTER IV.

PAGE

1. Measure of the number of vibrations ; the graphic method—2. Cagniard de la Tour's siren—3. Pitch of sounds ; limit of audible sounds, of musical sounds and of the human voice—4. The "normal pitch"—5. Laws of the vibrations of a string, and of harmonics 59

CHAPTER V.

1. Musical sounds—2. Law of simple ratio—3. Unison, interference—4. Beats—5. Their explanation—6. Resultant notes—7. Octaves and other harmonics—8. Consonant chords and their limits—9. The major fifth, fourth, sixth, and third ; the minor third and sixth—10. The seventh harmonic 74

CHAPTER VI.

1. Helmholtz's double siren—2. Application of the law of simple ratio to three or more notes—3. Perfect major and minor chords, their nature—4. Their inversion 96

CHAPTER VII.

1. Discords—2 and 3. The nature of music and musical scales—4. Ancient music—5. Greek scale—6. Scale of Pythagoras 7. Its decay—8. Ambrosian and Gregorian chants—9. Polyphonic music, harmony, the Protestant Reformation, Palestrina—10. Change of the musical scale, the tonic, and fundamental chord—11. The major scale, musical intervals

PAGE

—12. The minor scale—13. Key and transposition—14 and 15. Sharps and flats—16. The temperate scale, its inaccuracy—17. Desirability of abandoning it . . . 109

CHAPTER VIII.

1. Quality or *timbre* of musical sounds—2. Forms assumed by the vibrations, optical method—3. Another optical method —4. Phonautographic method—5. Laws of harmonics.—6. Quality or *timbre* of strings and of instruments—7. General laws of chords—8. Noises accompanying musical sounds—9. Quality or *timbre* of vocal musical sounds . . 146

CHAPTER IX.

1. Difference between science and art—2. Italian and German music—3 and 4. Separation of the two schools—5. Influence of Paris—6. Conclusion 175

THE THEORY OF SOUND.

CHAPTER I.

1. Periodic movements, vibration—2. Sonorous vibration—3. Vibration of a bell—4. Vibration of a tuning-fork, graphic method—5. Vibration of a string—6. Of plates and membranes—7. Vibration of air in a sounding pipe—8. Method by the manometric flame.—9. Conclusion.

1. Amongst the innumerable forms of motion which exist in nature, the science of Physics pays especial attention to some, to which it assigns great importance. These are those forms of motion in which a body, or part of a body, arrives at an extreme point, remains at rest for a moment, retraces its steps, again takes the road it has already passed over, and continues thus, making regular to-and-fro movements in a determinate line.

The pendulum offers us the most simple example of such a periodic movement. Its laws have been determined by Galileo, who discovered that the movement is isochronous—that is to say, that the time in which the to-and-fro movement is executed, is always the same for the same pendulum, be its oscillations large or not.

In other words, if we give to a pendulum at rest a slight impulse, or a strong impulse, the oscillations will be respectively small or large; but for the same pendulum the duration of each oscillation will be always the same; which may be expressed as follows, that the duration of the oscillations is independent of their extent.

The law of the isochronism of the pendulum is a very general law in nature. Although it may not be mathematically exact, still it is sufficiently so for the majority of cases which we shall consider. Every periodic to-and-fro movement comparable with that of the pendulum is called an oscillation, and if it be smaller and quicker, it is also termed a vibration. For greater clearness we will give the name of *simple vibrations* to those which exactly follow the laws of the pendulum, which, by the way, are the most simple of all. On the other hand, we will give the name of *compound vibrations* to those which follow more complex laws.

An example will show how vibrations can be more complex. The movement of the pendulum may be thus summed up: When it has arrived at the end of its path, it remains at rest for a moment, and comes back with a constantly-increasing velocity, which becomes a maximum in the vertical position, and then decreases during the second half of its path. For the pendulum, then, the two extreme points of the oscillation correspond to a velocity zero, the middle point to the maximum velocity.

An example of compound periodic movement is obtained

by adding to the already existing oscillation of the pendulum some other oscillatory movement. Suppose, for example, that the pendulum rod be flexible and elastic, and that it oscillates on its own account, and let us further suppose the lower heavy part of the pendulum to be an elastic ball, which, being violently impelled when at rest, vibrates like a ball on a billiard-table—that is to say, exhibits successive compressions and expansions. We shall then have three vibratory movements united in the pendulum, which will give a *compound* movement obviously more complex than the first.

Another example of a compound movement is furnished by the ball-player, who throws a ball vertically up in the air, and then sends it up again without allowing it to fall to the ground. Here the movement is different from that of the pendulum. The ball goes up with a velocity decreasing nearly at the same rate as that of the pendulum does (but the velocity decreases according to a different law), comes to rest, and then falls with a constantly-increasing velocity, and is suddenly stopped and thrown up again by the muscular force of the player, whilst its velocity is fairly high and still increasing, according to the laws which regulate the falling of heavy bodies. In this case, then, contrary to that which takes place in that of the pendulum, the two extreme points of the path correspond —the one to a velocity of zero, the other to a fairly high velocity—in fact, to the highest velocity possible under the circumstances. There exist in nature a very great number of vibrations of various forms, and that these have been carefully studied and their importance fully understood, constitutes one of the most pregnant strides which Physics has made in this century.

Of all these vibratory movements I will treat of one group, which merits special attention on account of the great facility which it offers for its study, and for the great importance which its application has exercised on the history of human culture.

2. I wish first of all to demonstrate that sound is formed by the vibrations of the particles of bodies. To understand these vibrations we are not obliged to know the intimate structure of the bodies themselves; it is enough to know that the body can be subdivided into little particles, and that these particles can move away from one another, at least within certain limits, without thereby causing the rupture or disaggregation of the body. This is the result of everyday observation, and in regard to our present study, I have no need to go farther into the matter or to formulate a more or less hypothetical opinion on the intimate structure of the bodies themselves. We must, however, add to this conception yet another—that of the elasticity of bodies. A body is called elastic in which a particle, moved from its natural position of equilibrium, has a tendency to return to its first position as soon as the external cause which had displaced it has ceased.

When a particle is under the circumstances here contemplated, it does what the pendulum does. The instant it is free to move, it returns towards the position it originally occupied; at first with small velocity, afterwards with constantly-increasing velocity. Arrived at its position of natural equilibrium, it continues for a certain space by its momentum the movement which it has acquired, and finally stops and retraces its steps. It oscillates then about its position of natural equilibrium, precisely as the pendulum oscillates on one side and the other of its vertical position. Mathematical investigation shows that in this case the vibration is simple, like that of the pendulum. But in the study of the vibrations to which a body, or part of a body, may be subjected, it is not enough to consider the movement of one particle only. The body is formed of a vast number of particles, and as each one vibrates, it is important to know whether they influence each other in their respective movements. In this respect any case is possible, according to the special conditions under which the vibrations take place, and the cause which excites them. It often happens that each single particle vibrates on its own account, as if the others were not in existence. Those vibrations which take place irregularly in all possible directions, acquire a great importance in respect to the phenomena of heat, and for others besides, but have no direct bearing upon sound. In order that the vibration may be sonorous, it is necessary that the particles should execute their movements together and with a certain regularity. The vibrations then acquire a general and regular character. They may be compared to the compact manœuvres of a company of soldiers, while the thermal vibrations rather resemble the altogether irregular movements of an undisciplined crowd.

3. It can be demonstrated by a certain number of examples that sound is always accompanied by vibration of the sounding body. A metal bell is taken, mouth upwards, firmly attached to a foot A (fig. 1). A very light

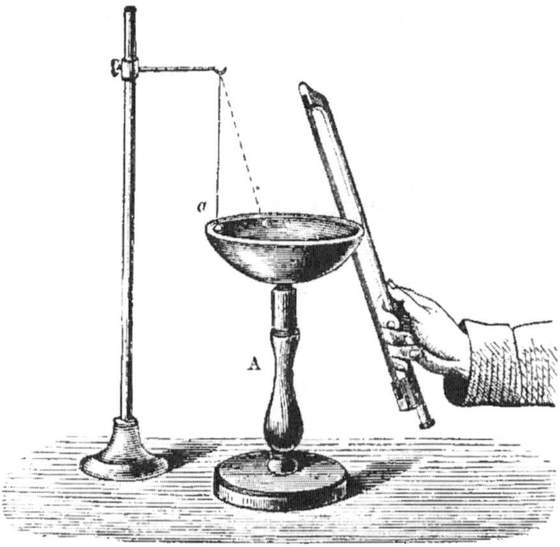

Fig. 1.

pendulum *a* touches the bell to indicate the movements that it may make at a given moment. If this bell be rubbed by a violin bow, a very marked sound is obtained, and immediately the pendulum is driven away, falls back against the bell, and is again driven away, and so on; the movement of the pendulum lasts for a certain time, and grows less as the sound dies away, and shows that the bell, so long as it sounds, is in a state of vibration in all its parts.

4. Another illustration is given by a sort of steel fork D, which, if it be held by its foot, can be easily set in vibration (fig. 2). A fork of this kind is called a tuning-fork. If the tuning-fork be struck upon the table, or if it be rubbed at the extremities of its branches with a violin bow, a very faint and scarcely audible musical sound is obtained. This sound is observably strengthened if the foot of the tuning-fork be placed in contact with the table, or, better still, with a hollow box. The sound can then be clearly heard, and by this means it may be shown that the sound really exists. This being so, it is easy to believe that the two branches of the tuning-fork, when it sounds, are in a state of continual vibratory movement. The movement is very rapid and the eye cannot follow it, but the outlines of the branches no longer have a sharp and well-defined form, which clearly shows the movement of the tuning-fork. This vibratory movement is made very perceptible by touching the fork itself with the finger. If the two branches be touched, the movement ceases, and with it the sound. Sound and movement are so correlated that one is strong when the other is strong, one diminishes when the other diminishes, and the one stops when the other stops.

But the vibrations of the tuning-fork can be made visible by the following graphic method:—

A plate of glass L (fig. 2), coated with lamp-black by a petroleum flame, and which slides easily in the frame G, is taken, and a point P having been attached to one of

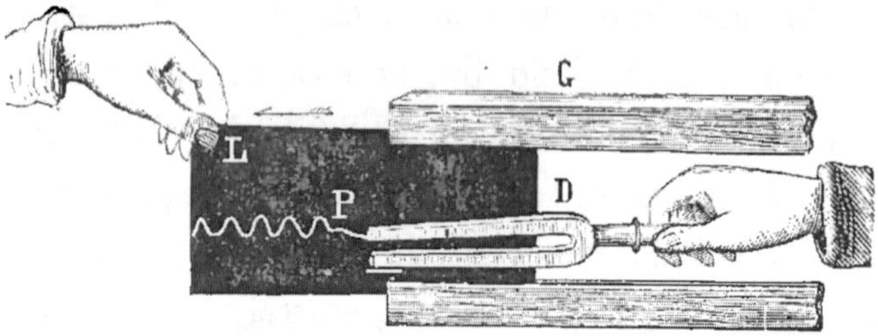

Fig. 2.

the branches of the vibrating tuning-fork, this point is placed against it, and the plate is drawn along rapidly in such a way that the point slides continuously on it.

Or, to make the experiment still more certain and more elegant, a cylinder of brass is used, on which is stretched a sheet of paper blackened by a petroleum flame. This cylinder can be turned by means of a screw handle A moved by hand or by mechanism (fig. 3). The tuning-fork is now brought close to the cylinder, so that the point D slightly scores the paper, and is fixed firmly by means of a vice. If the tuning-fork remains at rest and the cylinder turns, the point traces a straight line on the paper, or, as the movement of the cylinder is spiral, it traces a curve differing very little from a straight line.

If, on the other hand, the cylinder remains at rest and the tuning-fork vibrates, its point traces a short line perpendicular to the first. If, lastly, the tuning-fork vibrates and the cylinder turns, a regular and very characteristic undulating line is obtained on the paper, which represents fairly well the vibratory movement of the tuning-fork. When the tuning-fork gives a loud sound, the vibrations

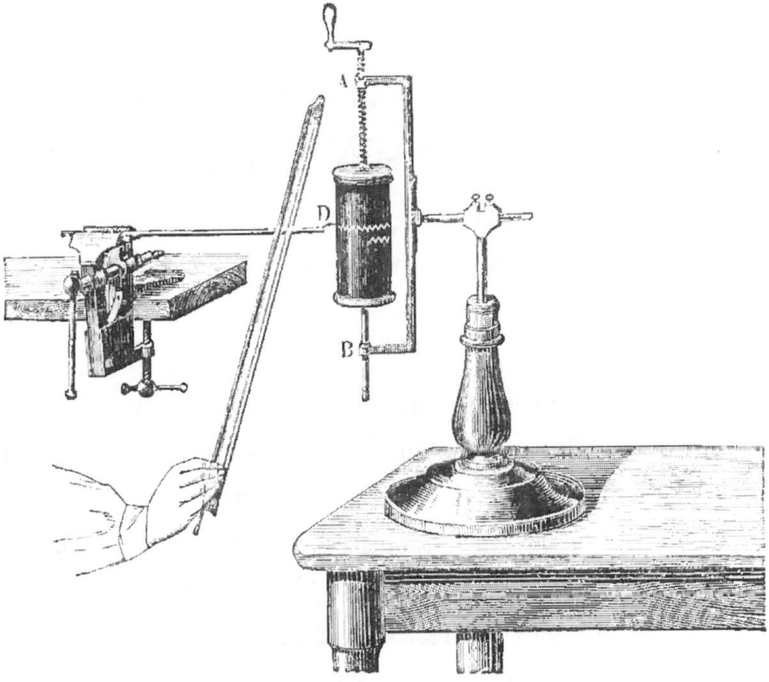

Fig. 3.

traced on the paper are very wide; later on, when the sound is already weakened, the vibrations begin to diminish in width; finally, when the sound is on the point of ceasing, they become almost invisible, and are sensibly confounded with the straight line.

5. The vibration of a string can also be very easily demonstrated. For this purpose a metal string is used, stretched over a wooden box (fig. 4). Two bridges, A and

B, on which the string rests, give it the exact length of one metre, and a scale placed beneath it enables the length of any part to be determined at will. The wire is fixed

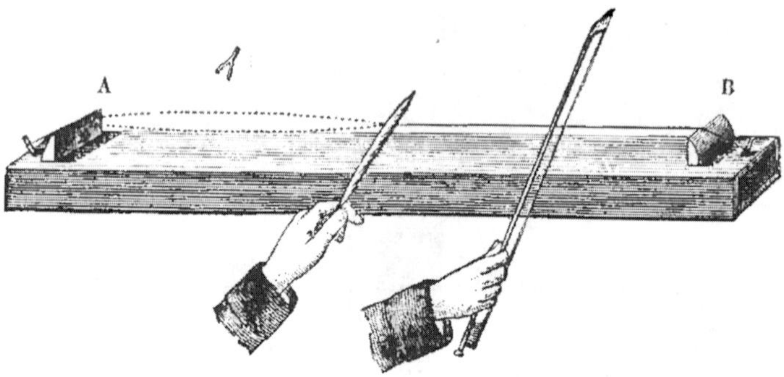

Fig. 4.

and kept stretched by means of pegs, exactly as in a pianoforte. This instrument, which has been known since the days of the ancient Greeks, and which is called a *sonometer* or *monochord*, is of great importance both in the history of music and in the study of those phenomena in which we are now interested. If the string be rubbed in the middle with a violin bow, a note is obtained, the pitch of which depends on many circumstances, as, for instance, on the length, thickness, and density of the string, and on its tension. If the string be rubbed lightly, the sound is feeble; if, on the contrary, it be rubbed with some force, the sound is loud; and, generally speaking, the intensity or loudness of the sound depends on the greater or less amount of force that produces it. The vibration of this string can be demonstrated in the following manner:—

Simple observation has already shown that the string

when rubbed is in a state of rapid vibration. At the extremities, where it rests on the two bridges, the string appears to be at rest, but when the middle part is examined, it is found that the string loses its sharpness of outline. It appears sensibly thickened, and this thickening reaches its maximum at about the middle of the string, which proves that each particle of the string performs a to-and-fro movement in a direction perpendicular to the length of the string. Vibrations of this sort are called *transverse*, to distinguish them from *longitudinal* vibrations, in which each particle vibrates in the direction of the string itself.

In practical music no use is made of the longitudinal vibration of strings; the transverse vibrations only need here be treated of. In order better to demonstrate their existence, some little slips of paper, doubled in the middle like riders, may be placed on the string; when it vibrates, these riders are thrown up on account of their lightness and fall back again on the string, thus indicating when it is in a state of vibration and when it is at rest. The most simple form of vibration is that in which the whole string performs simultaneously one single vibration. This effect can easily be obtained by leaving the string quite free, and rubbing it with the bow close to one of its ends. In that case all the riders are thrown up—first those in the middle, where the movement is greatest, and afterwards the others in succession. This shows that, with the exception of the two fixed points of the string, there is no point of it that does not vibrate, or, in other terms, that the whole string vibrates in one single vibration. The note which is thus obtained from the string is the lowest note corresponding to it, and it is for this reason that it is called its *fundamental* note.

But this is not the only note which can be obtained from the string. If it be touched at its middle with the finger, or, better still, with a feather (fig. 4), a note is obtained which is observably higher—a note which the musical ear easily distinguishes, and which practical musicians call the *octave* of the fundamental note. The string in this case vibrates in two parts in such a way that the point touched remains at rest. This fixed point is called a *node* of the vibrating string, and such a node has been produced artificially by touching the string at the point indicated. In fact, if the riders be now placed on the string, it will be observed in this case that the rider nearest to the finger does not move, whilst all the others are thrown off. The rider by remaining at rest thus indicates the presence of the node. Successively higher and higher notes can be obtained from the string by touching it at a third, a fourth, and a fifth of its length, &c. An experiment made by means of riders shows that in each case of this sort the string subdivides itself into a certain number of parts, invariably equal—in the first case into three, in the second into four, and in the third into five, &c.—and the riders that remain on the string will indicate the equidistant nodes formed in the string. Thus, for example, if the string be touched at one-fifth of its length, it divides itself into five equal parts, and four nodes are formed at distances of $\frac{1}{5}$, $\frac{2}{5}$, $\frac{3}{5}$, $\frac{4}{5}$ of the string's length, whilst at the intermediate points is

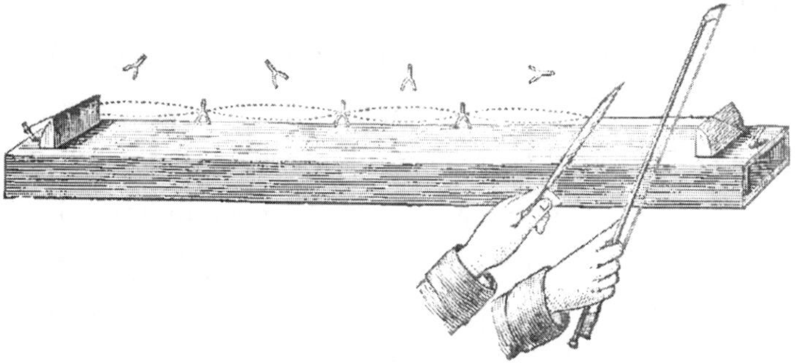

Fig. 5.

found the maximum vibratory movement (fig. 5). The parts of the string between the nodes which contain these points of maximum movement are called *ventral segments.*

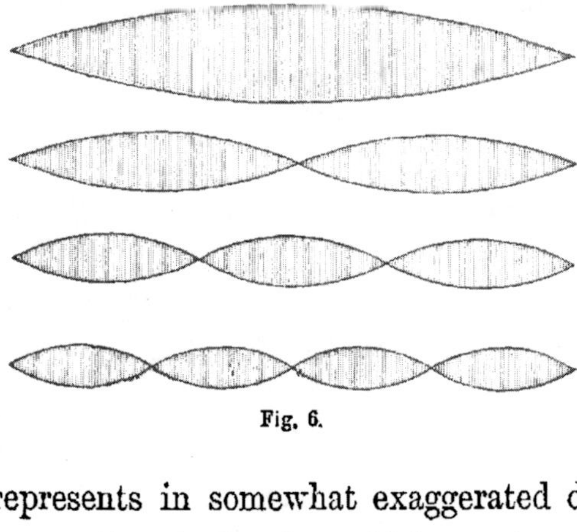

Fig. 6.

Fig. 6 represents in somewhat exaggerated dimensions the different modes of vibration which a string assumes in different cases, when it vibrates as a whole, or is divided into 2, 3, 4, &c., parts. In the first case no node is formed, in the others we have 1, 2, 3, &c., nodes. It is necessary to observe that these different cases correspond to different, and successively higher and higher, notes of the same string.

6. Another interesting example of vibration is that offered by a plate or membrane. This case is somewhat more complicated than that of a string, but the explanation is almost the same. In fact, a plate may be considered as an assemblage of strings rigidly fastened together. As we obtained nodal points in the string, we ought therefore to have nodal lines in the plate, formed by the junction of the different nodal points.

Chladni, who first observed these nodal lines, indicated a very simple means of demonstrating them, on which account the figures produced by these lines are called "Chladni's figures." Fig. 7 shows some plates, such as are

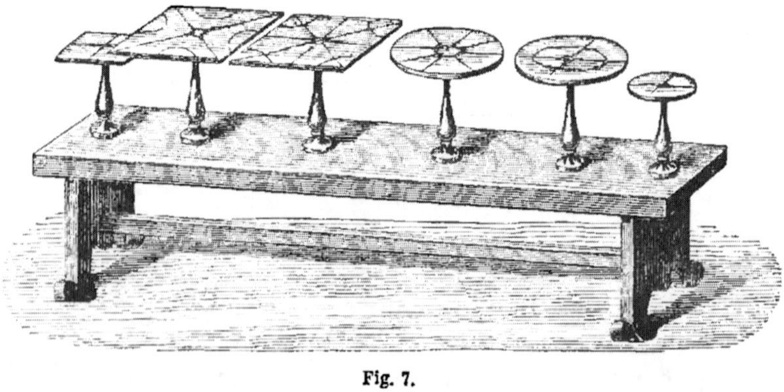

Fig. 7.

generally used, fixed in the middle to a solid foot, which rests on a common bench. By sprinkling a little sand on the plate and rubbing it with a bow, musical sounds are obtained, unpleasant because too shrill, but always quite clear; and the moment the sound is produced, the sand dances about and collects together on certain straight or curved lines, which indicate the places where the vibratory movement does not exist: these are Chladni's nodal lines.

From the same plate very varied figures can be obtained

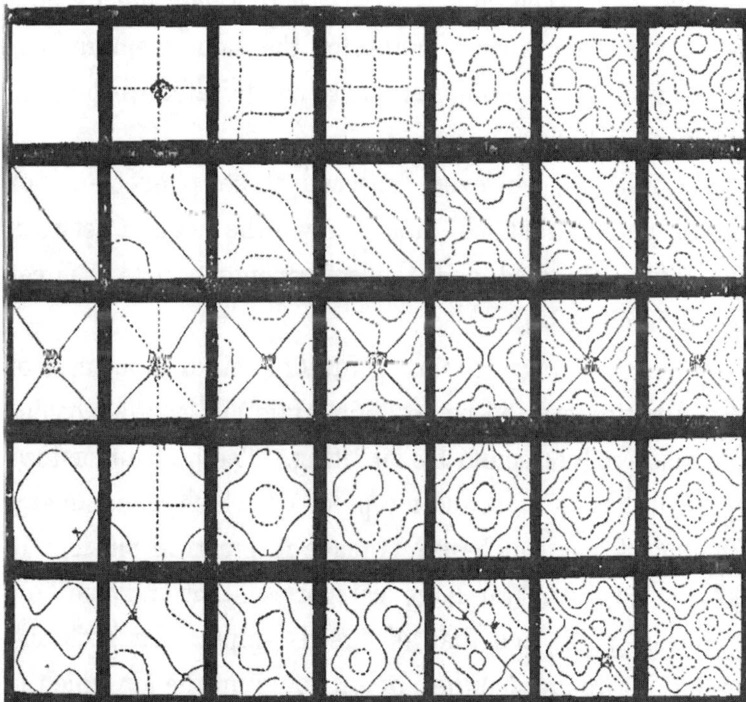

Fig. 8.

by applying the finger to suitable points, in order thus to induce a nodal point, and thence a nodal line. Fig. 8

contains a very beautiful series of figures, which can be obtained, according to *Savart*, from a square plate of sufficient size. The number of these figures is rather large, and those here drawn represent only a small part of those which can be obtained, especially when the plate is large.

Membranes also vibrate in an analogous way. The forms of their nodal lines are generally even more complicated than those of plates, and are observed in an analogous way. The rule is this, that to a determinate note belongs a determinate figure for the same membrane or plate, and that the figure is more complicated as the note produced is higher.

No relation, however, between these phenomena, or rather no law that will make known the relation between the figure obtained and the corresponding note, has yet been discovered.

7. We have up to this point only studied the case of the vibration of solid bodies, but liquid and gaseous bodies can also produce sound by vibrating. The best-understood case is that of a sounding pipe, of which under many different forms much use is made in practical music. It is divided into two large categories—that of "flue" or "mouth" pipes, and that of "reed" pipes. In both the sound is produced either by breaking up the air which is blown into them, or by causing it to enter in puffs. In the first and most important—that is, in the flue-pipe—this effect is obtained by a special arrangement, which is called the embouchure of the pipe.

Fig. 9 represents the most common form of flue-pipe. By blowing through the open tube *a*, whether by means of the mouth or by connecting the pipe to a bellows, a musical sound is obtained. The pipe is hollow within, and open or closed at the top, according to circumstances, and it has its embouchure at *m* and *l*. Fig. 10 shows better

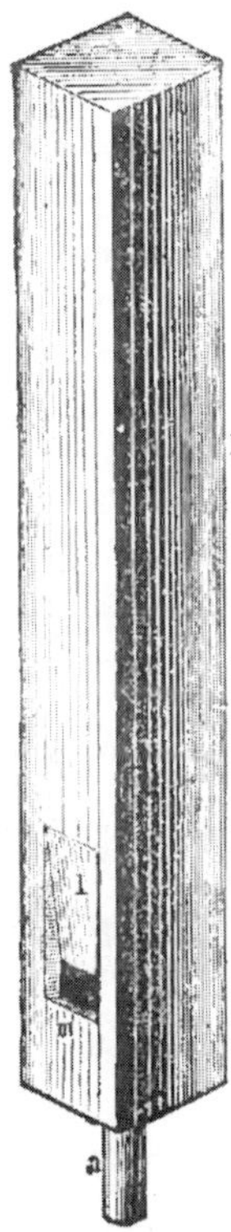

Fig. 9.

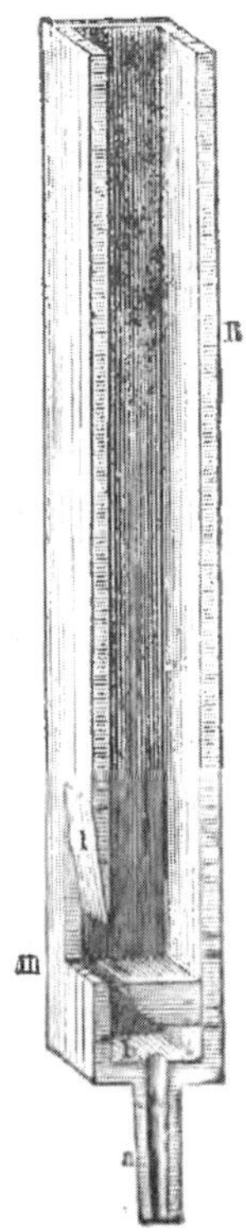

Fig. 10.

in section the arrangement of such an embouchure, which consists of an upper lip *l* and a lower lip *m*, which are bevelled to an edge. The air enters by the tube *a*, passes into the box *b*, and breaks through a narrow fissure against the upper lip *l*. It partly enters the pipe, and induces vibrations, and produces a very clear and agreeable sound.

Fig. 11 gives an example of a *reed* pipe. The air, which enters by *r*, is obliged, in order to get to the larger tube R, to pass through a special apparatus, *the reed*, of which fig. 12

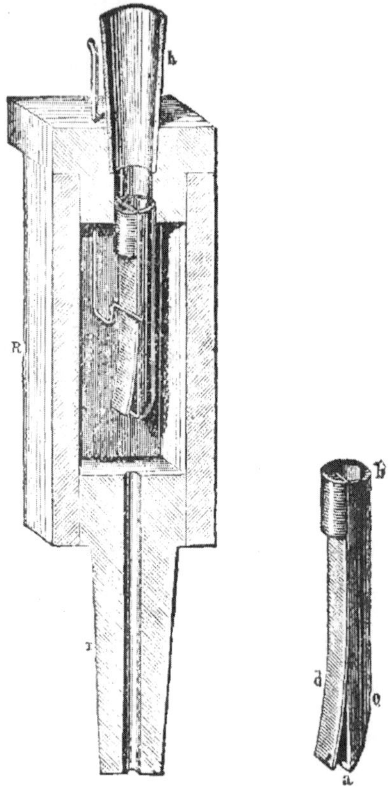

Fig. 11. Fig. 12.

gives the detailed arrangement. The box *acb* is closed in the middle by a small, thin, elastic, metallic plate *d*, called the tongue. When this is lifted up, the air passes through the fissure *a*; when the tongue springs back by its own elasticity, it closes the passage. The vibration of the tongue induces a rapid opening and closing of this fissure; the air penetrates at intervals, in regular puffs, and thus a sound is obtained. Whether the first or second kind of pipe be used, if we blow hard the sound is loud; it becomes feeble if we blow gently, and in this last case the note is the lowest that the pipe can give, for which reason it is called the fundamental note of the pipe.

This note depends on the dimensions, and, above all, on the length of the pipe, and also on the nature of the gas that enters it; so that to determinate dimensions and to a determinate mode of blowing corresponds a determinate fundamental note. When the blowing is stronger, it may happen that the pipe will give a different note from the fundamental note. This happens especially if the pipe is very narrow for its length; it is easy to prevent this by giving to the tube a sectional area proportioned to its length, according to certain rules suggested by practice.

A pipe, then, may be constructed at pleasure which will give by preference the fundamental note, or one which will give by preference higher notes. Sometimes the one case and sometimes the other is utilised in practical music.

In fact there are instruments, both with embouchures and with reeds, in which each pipe is intended only to give its fundamental note—as, for example, the organ, in all the various and complicated forms which it can assume. Many wind instruments—as the trumpet, trombone, &c., and also the flute—are pipes, each one of which is intended to give a series of notes. This is attained by giving the instruments great length in proportion to their other dimensions and turning and twisting the pipe when too long in order to give it a more convenient form. Like a vibrating string, a sounding pipe thus gives a series of notes successively higher and higher. It is enough for this to strengthen the current of air; but a better and quicker effect is obtained by opening a communication with the external air at suitable points by means of *pistons* in the cornet, and by means of the fingers and of the *keys* in the flute. The effect may be compared with that obtained when a point in a vibrating string is touched by the finger; a node is established, and the vibrating column of air subdivides into a certain number of parts, according to simple rules, which vary, however, with the nature of the pipe.

The flute and organ pipes for the most part are flue-pipes, but in the first the embouchure is formed both by the instrument itself and the lip of the player. The clarionet, the oböe, and all the trumpet class, are reed instruments; these last have a little funnel against which the lips are placed, which by vibrating act as a reed.

All the various different-shaped pipes are divided into open and stopped. Besides certain very characteristic differences, the note produced by the two kinds of pipes is, *cæteris paribus,* different in pitch. Two pipes of the same shape and dimensions, the one stopped and the other open, give two fundamental notes which are to each other as the fundamental note and its octave. If therefore an open pipe be stopped, its note descends to the octave below; and if a stopped pipe be opened, its note rises to the octave above.

Many different methods may be used to demonstrate the vibration of air in a pipe. One method is to introduce into an open pipe, one wall of which is of glass, by its upper end a light, well-stretched membrane of paper *m* on which some sand is sprinkled (fig. 13). The note is slightly altered by the introduction of this extraneous body, but nevertheless continues to exist, and through the glass wall it may be observed how the sand is thrown up with some noise, because the vibration of the air is communicated to the paper membrane and thence to the sand. At the middle point of the pipe the movement of the sand ceases, which shows that at this point there is a true node, and also that the dancing of the sand is not produced by air in a stream, but only by air in a state of vibration.

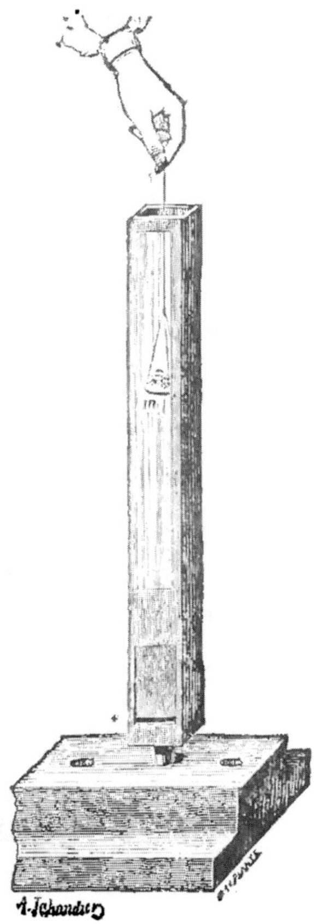

Fig. 13.

Another simple mode of demonstrating the vibration

of the air is the following: A tube rather long for its sectional area is taken, in which one wall is made of very thin flexible wood. By blowing into it with some violence, a note is obtained much higher than the fundamental note of the pipe. The air in vibrating communicates its vibrations to the flexible side of the tube. Therefore, if the pipe be held horizontally, and sand be sprinkled on the flexible side, the sand will dance about and accumulate in certain lines which are true nodal lines, and indicate exactly the way in which the air is vibrating in the interior of the pipe.

Another method of some importance has been pointed out by Kundt. Take a tube of glass of sufficient sectional area and about two metres long. Some light powder, such as lycopodium or cork dust, is poured into the interior of the tube, and distributed over it fairly evenly. The tube is then stopped at the two extremities with corks; it is then held firmly by its middle with one hand, whilst it is rubbed with a slightly wetted cloth with the other. A very sharp clear note is then formed; the vibrations of

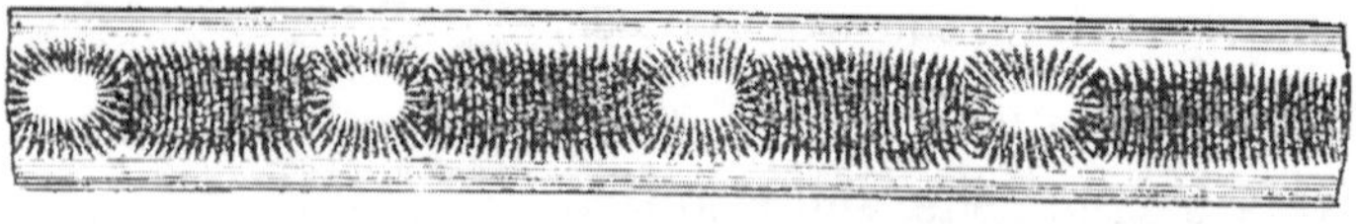

Fig. 14.

the tube are transmitted to the enclosed air, and the light powder distributes itself regularly in the way indicated in fig. 14, where a portion of the tube is represented. The circles are nodes, and between them the powder shows real transverse lines.

The form of the figure, and especially the distribution of the nodes, depends on various circumstances—on the dimensions of the tube, on the note which can consequently be obtained from it, and on the gas which is enclosed in the tube. In this respect Kundt's method is susceptible of great accuracy, and is widely applicable, enabling us to deduce the velocity with which sound is propagated through different bodies.

8. The mechanician *König* has recently devised a very elegant novel method of demonstrating the vibrations of the air in sounding pipes—viz., that by means of the manometric flame. Fig. 15 gives a sufficiently exact idea of the apparatus contrived by him. One or more pipes, equal or unequal (in the annexed drawing they are equal A and B), are mounted on a small box *b*, which acts as an air-chest. The indiarubber tube *a* puts it in communication with a blower. The valves *v* serve to set in action at will either pipe or both together. In the pipe itself a hole is made and closed again by a capsule *e*, under which is a flexible elastic membrane which serves to separate the interior of the pipe from the interior of the capsule, which is put in communication on one side with a gas-tube *c* by means of the small tube *d*, and on the other with the small tube *f*, which ends in a gas-burner. The gas then enters the capsule, fills it, and passes through the small tube and the burner. Lighting it, then, at the burner,

a small flame is obtained. If the pipe is not sounding, the gas passes quietly through the capsule, and gives rise to a quiet and normal flame. If, on the other hand, the pipe

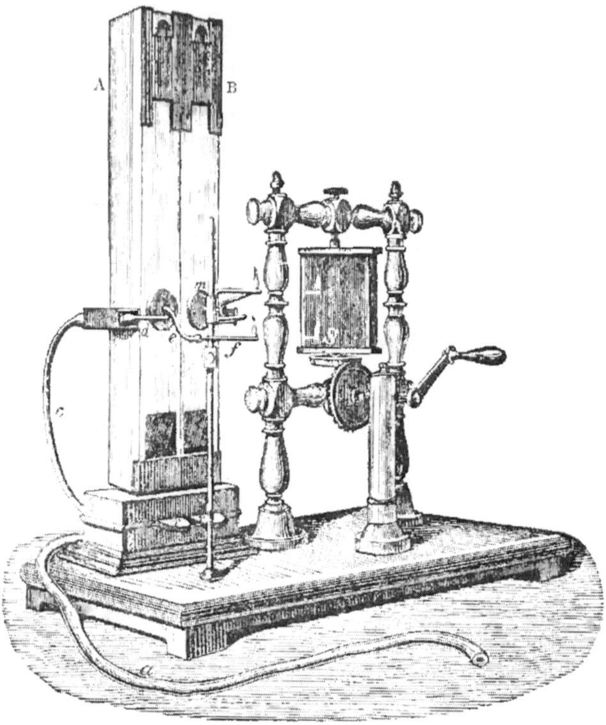

Fig. 15.

produces its note, the movement of the vibrating air is communicated to the membrane, from it to the gas, and thence to the flame. When the pipe produces this note, it will be seen that the flame lengthens, grows restless and more blue, and by all its behaviour indicates something abnormal. This proceeds from the fact that the flame takes part in the vibrations of the air in the pipe.

It rises and falls rapidly, and as this movement, on account of its rapidity, cannot be followed by the eye, only a complete image of the flame is seen, an image caused by the superposition of the partial short and long flames.

In order readily to observe the vibrations of the flame, recourse is had to a means often made use of in physics. Behind the flames is placed a four-sided box of looking-glass S, which can be rapidly turned round a vertical axis by means of a handle and a system of toothed wheels. When the flame burns steadily, a continuous luminous band is formed in the turning mirror, because to each position which the mirror takes up in its rotation, there corresponds a similar image of the flame. If, on the other hand, the flame vibrates—that is to say, if it is sometimes short and sometimes long—there will correspond to certain positions of the mirror long, and to others short images, and there will be seen in the turning mirror long and short images succeeding each other (fig. 16, *a*).

The short flame is confounded sensibly with the luminous mass, because the lower part of the flame does not take much part in the vibrations. But the long flames are seen clearly separated one from the other; whence the phenomenon presents the appearance of separate and equal flames, as is shown in fig. 16. This method gives a clear idea of what happens in the interior of the pipe, and if

Fig. 16.

care be taken to darken the room in order to remove all other reflections from the mirror, the experiment becomes perfectly visible even to a very numerous audience. A smaller pipe may now be used, which gives a note exactly an octave higher than that of the first.

When the apparatus is set in action in the same way as at first, it will be observed that the vibrating flames are considerably nearer together. In general terms, *the higher the note*, for an equal speed of the mirror, the nearer together are the flames—that is to say, *the more rapid are the vibrations of the air in the pipe.* This is a very important law, which will require further study later on, but which it is useful to have already demonstrated by this elegant experiment. We may even go farther, and determine the ratio between the number of vibrations per second of the two pipes. Setting them both in action independently of each other, two series of flames are obtained one over the other (fig. 16, *a b*). And with a little attention it will be seen that with whatever velocity the mirror be turned, two images of the lower line correspond to one image of the upper line. This conclusion may then be arrived at, *that the octave is always composed of a number of vibrations per second double that of the fundamental note.*

9. Similar demonstrations might be continued, for, in truth, examples are not wanting. A few only of the more important have been cited, and these will suffice to demonstrate the point to be settled in this chapter. Wherever

there is sound, there is always vibration; whence it may be concluded that sound and vibration are concomitant phenomena. The vibration may come from a solid, a liquid, or a gaseous body; but there is no known case of sound, without vibration of material bodies. It does not necessarily follow that all vibrations must produce sound. In order that this may happen, they must satisfy certain special conditions, which will be considered later on. But up to this point we may say, that wherever there is sound there is vibration. But vibration is objective: it exists in sounding bodies independently of the listener.

Sound, on the other hand, is produced in our ears, and is therefore subjective. To a deaf man the vibration exists, but the sound does not. He would be able to study the vibration, though entirely ignorant of the fact that it produces a special sensation on our normal organisation. From this we may conclude that *vibration is the cause and sound the effect* produced on our ears, or in other words, that sound is the result of certain forms of vibration of bodies.

CHAPTER II.

1. Transmission of sound—2. Propagation in air—3. In water and other bodies—4. Velocity of sound in air—5. In water and other bodies—6. Reflection of sound—7. Echo.

1. We possess in our organisation a special instrument, the ear, adapted for perceiving sounds. But if the vibrations of the sounding body are the cause of sound, the question arises, How do these vibrations ultimately reach our ears, so as to produce the sensation of sound? A vibration evidently could not be propagated if there were no medium fit to propagate it. This medium is generally air; but it may also be any other solid, liquid, or gaseous body, so long as it be elastic. Elasticity of the body is a necessary condition, not only for the formation of sound, but also for its transmission: since a vibration can only be propagated by transmitting its own movement to the layers of the medium nearest the vibrating body; these layers communicate it to fresh layers in their neighbourhood, and so on.

Vibration seems, then, to travel from layer to layer, and when circumstances permit, in every direction. The vibratory movement is not possible if each particle of the transmitting medium be not able to vibrate on its own account—that is to say, if the medium be not elastic. And thus the power that a body possesses of transmitting sound constitutes one of the surest criteria of its elasticity.

A very clear idea of the transmission of a vibratory movement may be obtained by observing a large surface of water at rest. On throwing a stone into it, a series of concentric waves is seen to start from the point struck by the stone, which as they grow larger, become less distinct, and end by becoming imperceptible. It would be a mistake to suppose that the water itself moved from point to point. Each particle remains, so to speak, at its post, and only executes a vibration perpendicular to the direction of the wave; having accomplished which, it is at the very same post as before. It is easy to demonstrate that this is so, by throwing on the water some sawdust or other floating body, when it will be observed that it is lifted by the vibratory movement which passes under it, without being sensibly displaced. It is, then, only the vibratory movement which moves from one point to another, and not the body itself or any part of it.

The case of several vibratory movements, which coming from different points strike against or across each other, is more complicated, and at the same time more interesting. If two or more stones be thrown into still water at different points, two or more systems of waves are formed, which, as they grow larger, join together. Experience shows that at each point common to two waves moving in opposite directions, there are special phenomena, called *interference.* But beyond these points, each wave is propagated exactly as if the other did not exist, and never had existed.

This is the great principle of the *coexistence* of vibratory movements, a principle discovered by experiment and proved to demonstration by mathematical analysis. It is applicable to all cases, whatever be the elastic body examined, and whatever be the nature of its vibrations. Applied to the case of sonorous vibrations and air, it leads to this conclusion: that twenty, thirty, a hundred different sounds may be transmitted in every direction without reciprocal disturbance.

2. In order to demonstrate that air is really able to transmit sound, use is made of a glass globe, into which a rod of brass penetrates, carrying at its lower extremity a little bell *c* (fig. 17) attached by means of an inelastic cotton thread. The globe is furnished with a stopcock *a* in its neck, which enables it to be opened or closed. If the air be exhausted from the globe as thoroughly as possible by means of an air-pump, the globe, and thence the bell, may be shaken with any degree of violence without any sound being heard. By holding the ear, however, against the globe, a very feeble sound is heard, the reason of which is, that the air is not completely exhausted, and that the cotton thread by which the bell

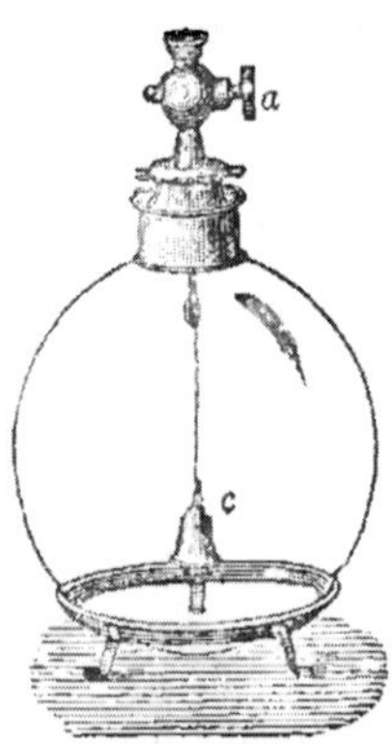

Fig. 17.

is suspended is not completely devoid of elasticity, and therefore transmits the sound, though but slightly. But the phenomenon is very faint, and is imperceptible at a very short distance. If the stopcock be opened for an instant and again closed, a little air will enter the globe, and the sound of the bell will begin to be heard. Its vibrations now find an elastic medium, which, although very rarefied, is able to transmit them at last to the glass envelope of the globe. The glass, which is very elastic, transmits them to the external air, and thence to the ear of the observer, and therefore the sound is heard, although feebly. If the stopcock be again opened, and left open so that the air can enter freely, the sound will grow louder, and when the air in the globe has reached the same density as the external air, the bell will be heard with its full loudness. This experiment shows that air is able to transmit sound, that in this case it was necessary for such transmission, and that it transmits sound better as its density is greater.

3. Not only air, but all solid, liquid, and gaseous bodies, are able, if elastic, to transmit sonorous vibrations. It is a well-known fact that if, when bathing in the sea, the head be plunged under water, or even the ears only, the noise produced by the water striking against the rocks is distinctly heard. And it is an equally well-known fact, that to hear a distant noise produced by the passage of men or animals, the ear must be held to the ground; which shows not only that the earth transmits

sound, but that in some cases it transmits it even better than air.

Almost all known bodies are able to transmit sound, and metals are best of all adapted for this purpose. This transmission succeeds best when the sound is circumscribed and obliged to travel in one direction only. This is not the case for a bell sounding in the open air; the sound is transmitted in every direction, and soon grows feeble. But if, on the other hand, the transmission takes place in one direction only, a sound, although feeble, may be heard at a great distance. It is on this principle that are founded the acoustic pipes, or *speaking-tubes*, in common use. These are cylindrical tubes, generally of gutta-percha, which are arranged from point to point as may be required, with this condition, however, that they should not have sharp curves. If words be spoken at one end, the sound is transmitted from layer to layer of the enclosed air, and easily reaches the other end; communication can thus be made between two distant parts of a building. Theoretically, there is no limit to such transmission in cylindrical tubes; in practice, however, the sound grows gradually weaker in long tubes, because the vibrating air loses a part of its vibratory movement by friction with the sides of the tube. Very long distances may nevertheless be attained.

An elegant experiment on the transmission of sound is that described by *Wheatstone.* A rod of wood several yards in length passes from one room to another—for example, from one room to the room on the floor below. In order to preserve it from contact with other bodies, it is surrounded by a tin tube and by indiarubber, but the two extremities are left free. One extremity is put in communication with the sounding-board of a pianoforte or other musical instrument, and transmits all its notes to the other extremity. To make these perceptible, it need only be fixed to some other instrument—a violin, harp, or pianoforte. The effect is astonishing; a piece of music played in the other room or other floor is perfectly heard.

4. This being so, the following questions now present themselves: With what velocity is sound transmitted in different bodies? Is it great or small? Is it the same for all bodies?

By velocity is meant the space passed over in a second of time; as an example, let us investigate the space passed over by a sonorous vibration in one second of time in air. It is a well-known fact that this velocity is not great. In fact, when a man some distance off strikes an anvil with a hammer, the movement of the hammer is first seen and then the sound is heard; and if the distance is rather great, the lapse of time between the moments at which the blow is seen and heard becomes very considerable. The firing of a cannon a long distance off is announced first by the flame produced by the explosion of the powder, and only some time afterwards by the report. Similar examples are very numerous. They demonstrate that sound is transmitted much more slowly than light, and that the velocity of sound in each case cannot be great.

The method of determining the velocity of sound is in itself very simple. It may be done by merely placing two cannon at two different stations as far apart as possible, and having exactly measured the distance between them, firing them at previously-arranged moments, and observing by means of a stop-watch the moment at which the report from the first station reaches the second, and *vice versâ*. The time which the sound takes to pass over the space comprised between the two stations is thus ascertained, and further, the distance between the two stations being also known, the required velocity is found by dividing the latter by the former. Such experiments must be made at night, so as not to be disturbed by other noises. They ought, further, to be made on calm nights when there is no wind, because wind, which is merely a change of place of a great mass of air, increases or diminishes the velocity of sound according as it is favourable or unfavourable—that is to say, according to whether its direction is the same as, or contrary to, the direction in which the sound is transmitted. But as it is impossible to be quite free from wind, the cannon are fired first from one station and then from the other, because in this case the wind will be favourable to the transmission of the one sound, and unfavourable to the transmission of the other. One of the two velocities will then be too great, the other too small, and the mean will represent a very close approximation to the value which would have been found had there been no wind.

Experiments of this kind have often been performed. We may note especially those made by members of the French Academy in the year 1822 between *Monthléry* and *Villejuif*, those made by *Moll* and *Van der Beck*, and lastly, those lately made by *Regnault* with much more perfect means.

The result of these experiments is, that the velocity of sound in air, at a temperature of 0° C. (32° F.), may be fixed in round numbers at 330 metres* in a second of time; and that this velocity increases regularly with the temperature, so that at a temperature of 16° C. (60·8° F.) it is about 340 metres per second. It was not at first known that it is rather greater for loud sounds than for feeble ones. However, this difference observed by *Regnault* is very small, and may be neglected in most cases. To confirm the influence of temperature on the velocity of sound, we may here notice the experiment made by Captain *Parry* in Melville Island, lying in the middle of the group of islands near North America, from which it results that for the very low temperature of 38·5° below zero C. (37·3° below 0° F.), the least velocity was 309 metres per second.

Another question is this, Are low and high notes propagated with the same velocity? Listening to a military band playing at a distance, it will be observed that the

* One metre is equal to 3·28 feet, *i.e.*, to about 3 feet 3 inches.

piece of music which is being executed completely preserves its rhythmic movement. The notes reach the observer enfeebled by a great distance, but they maintain exactly the same consecutive order. This, however, would not be possible if the different notes, whether high or low, had not the same velocity. *Biot* endeavoured to make more accurate experiments on this point by causing a known and very simple melody to be played on a flute in such a way that the sound entered one of the water-pipes at Paris. On listening at the other end of this very long pipe, he found the rhythm of the melody unaltered. It is not at all impossible that still more accurate experiments may reveal some such small difference in this respect as was found for loud and feeble sounds in certain of *Regnault's* experiments, but the difference would be certainly very small, and might in most cases be neglected.

5. The velocity of sound in water has been determined by *Colladon* and *Sturm* in the Lake of Geneva. A bell was suspended under water and sounded at known moments ; at a long distance from this a tube was led into the water from the boat, in which was the observer. The lower end of the tube was much enlarged, like a colossal ear, and was closed by means of an elastic membrane, which was completely under water. The sonorous vibrations from the bell were propagated through the water to the membrane, and from it to the air in the tube. The observer holding his ear to the tube, distinctly perceived

the sound. Whence, by measuring the distance from the bell to the observer, and the time occupied by the sound in traversing the whole distance, *Colladon* and *Sturm* found a velocity of 1435 metres per second. The velocity of sound through water is therefore appreciably greater than through air.

Many other experiments have been tried in order to arrive at the velocity of sound in different bodies. It would be impossible to enter into further details on these points without overstepping the limits I have laid down, the more so as the methods employed in these researches are very various, and require a somewhat profound knowledge of the theory of sound. I wish therefore to limit myself to the statement, that the velocity of sound is small in gaseous bodies, such as air, and is smaller in proportion as the gas is more dense; that it is therefore the smallest possible in carbonic anhydride [262 metres per second], which is a gas one and a half times denser than air, and the greatest possible in hydrogen [1269 metres per second], a gas which is fourteen times less dense than air. In gas an increase of temperature considerably increases the velocity.

In liquids the velocity is, generally speaking, sensibly greater than in gas [with the exception of hydrogen]. In solids it is found to be still greater, especially in metals, in which it rises as high as twenty times the velocity in air. But increase of temperature generally considerably diminishes the velocity, except in iron, in which at first the velocity increases with the temperature up to 100° C. (212° F.), and then rapidly diminishes.

These differences and these anomalies arise from the intimate structure of the various bodies, and from the way in which this structure varies with temperature. The velocity of sound depends on two quantities—on the elasticity and on the density of the body; it increases when the first increases and when the second diminishes. But as the laws according to which elasticity and density vary with the temperature are very various, especially in solid bodies, it follows that the variations of the velocity of sound in solids must also follow complicated laws.

For different kinds of wood there are very different values, according to the direction of the fibre and of the rings. The following table contains some results obtained in this respect, and will serve to render the above explanation more clear:—

VELOCITY OF SOUND IN VARIOUS BODIES.

					Metres per Second.
Air . .	at	0° C.	(32° F.),	according to sundry experimentalists	330
Oxygen .	„	0° C.	(32° F.),	according to Dulong .	317
Hydrogen .	„	0° C.	(32° F.)	„ „ .	1269
Carbonic anhydride	„	0° C.	(32° F.)	„ „ .	262
Common gas	„	0° C.	(32° F.)	„ „ .	314
Seine water	„	15° C.	(59° F.),	according to Wertheim	1437
Sea-water .	„	20° C.	(68° F.)	„ „ .	1453
Absolute alcohol	„	20° C.	(68° F.)	„ „ .	1160
Ethyl æther.	„	0° C.	(32° F.)	„ „ .	1159
Lead . .	„	20° C.	(68° F.)	„ „ .	1228
„ . .	„	100° C.	(212° F.)	„ „ .	1204

					Metres per Second.
Gold	at 20° C.	(68° F.),	according to	Wertheim	1743
„	„ 100° C.	(212° F.)	„	„	1719
„	„ 200° C.	(392° F.)	„	„	1634
Silver	„ 20° C.	(68° F.)	„	„	2707
„	„ 100° C.	(212° F.)	„	„	2639
„	„ 200° C.	(392° F.)	„	„	2477
Copper	„ 20° C.	(68° F.)	„	„	3556
„	„ 100° C.	(212° F.)	„	„	3292
„	„ 200° C.	(392° F.)	„	„	2954
Iron	„ 20° C.	(68° F.)	„	„	5127
„	„ 100° C.	(212° F.)	„	„	5299
„	„ 200° C.	(392° F.)	„	„	4719
Cast steel	„ 20° C.	(68° F.)	„	„	4986
„	„ 100° C.	(212° F.)	„	„	4925
„	„ 200° C.	(392° F.)	„	„	4788
Acacia wood along the fibre					4714
„ across the rings					1475
„ with the rings					1352
Pine in the direction of the fibre					3322
„ across the rings					1405
„ with the rings					794

6. When a sonorous wave strikes against an obstacle, it exhibits the same phenomena as an elastic body striking an elastic wall. The sonorous wave is reflected in such a way that the angle of incidence is equal to the angle of reflection. The angle formed by the ray of sound which impinges on the wall, with the perpendicular to the wall drawn from the point at which it impinges, is called the angle of incidence. The angle formed by this perpendicular with the reflected ray of sound is called the angle of reflection. By means of this law the direction taken by a ray of sound after its reflection can always be perfectly determined.

An innumerable quantity of phenomena of reflection exist. The two most distinct forms are resonance and echo. When a sound is produced in a closed chamber, the sonorous waves are propagated in every direction, strike against the walls of the chamber, and are sent back from them by reflection, and can be repeated several times from one wall to another. An observer within the chamber will hear not only the sound which comes direct from the sounding body, but will also receive the vibrations which come by reflection from all parts of the chamber.

The sound is thus remarkably strengthened, and this is the reason why it is easier to hear and to make one's self heard in a closed room than in an open space.

Evidently in such a case the sound will not only return strengthened, but even altered; because the reflections from the walls, on account of the low velocity of sound, require some time, and prolong the sound more or less considerably. If the chamber be small, this prolongation is not considerable and can be neglected; but when the chamber assumes large proportions—as, for example, in a theatre—each note spoken, sung, or played, may be considerably prolonged: it is confounded with the next note, and this phenomenon of resonance may become extremely troublesome unless it be remedied. This happens in all large, enclosed, empty places, where reflection takes place freely. There is only one way to prevent it, which consists in breaking up the large walls. The seats of a theatre, the decorations between them, the galleries, even the hangings, serve not merely for the accommodation of the spectators and for the internal beauty of the theatre, but also fill an even more important office—viz., that of preventing the disagreeable resonance of the place. It is one of the most difficult problems for an architect to construct a room on proper acoustic principles—that is to say, a room in which sound shall be considerably strengthened without degenerating into resonance, and it may be said that up to the present time this problem has been solved in very few theatres in a satisfactory way.

The reflection of sound has been utilised in various ways; nature and art have combined to solve some problems not deficient in interest. The celebrated "ear of Dionysius" is well known; it is a sort of hole excavated in the rocks near Syracuse, where the least sound is transformed into a deafening roar. The great dome of St Paul's Cathedral in London is so constructed that two persons at opposite points of the internal gallery, placed in the drum of the dome, can talk together in a mere whisper. The sound is transmitted from one to the other by successive reflections along the curve of the dome. Similar phenomena are often met with under the large arches of bridges, viaducts, &c.; and there was a period when problems of this nature were much sought after, and often solved, by architects. It is for this reason that whispering-galleries, speaking-pipes, &c., are so often met with in old houses.

An elegant mode of demonstrating the reflection of

sound is by the use of two parabolic reflectors MN M′N′ (fig. 18), placed one opposite the other in such a way that their centres shall be on the straight line AA′. Placing a sounding body at a particular point F, called the focus of the reflector MN, the sound-wave strikes against the reflector, is driven back thence by reflection on to the second

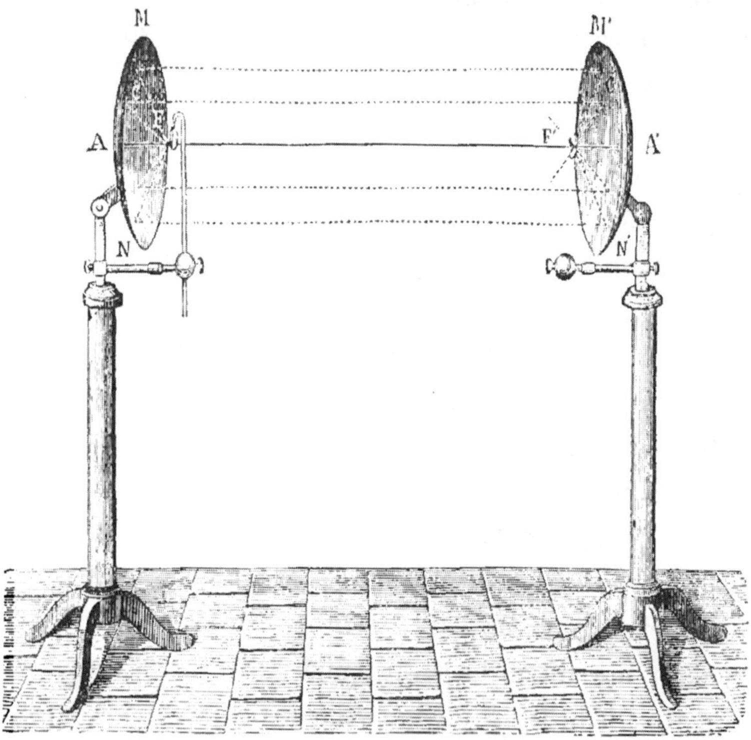

Fig. 18.

reflector, and by it is concentrated on to its own focus F′; that is to say, the ray FC is reflected in the direction CC′, and by a second reflection along C′F′. Each of the remaining rays is reflected in the same way, and they all concentrate at F′. An ear placed at this point distinctly perceives a very slight sound made at F, by means of the reflectors and of the double reflection which they give, whilst without the mirrors it would only be possible to perceive the ray FF′, which is much too feeble by itself to excite a sufficiently strong sensation.

Another case of multiple reflection is met with in the famous Baptistry at Pisa, a building surmounted by a narrow cupola of peculiar form. Placing one's self under the cupola inside the Baptistry and singing a note, the sound is prolonged for a very considerable time; therefore by singing three or four notes in cadence, by the effect of the reflections, a most beautiful chord is heard, as if from an organ, which is considerably prolonged.

7. The best understood of all the cases of reflection is that which is called *echo*. In order that an echo may be produced, it is necessary that there should be, at some distance from the observer, a large vertical wall, or some other object—as, for example, a rock—which roughly resembles a wall. A sound sent by the observer towards the wall returns from it by reflection, and if the distance passed over by the sound be sufficiently great, the reflected sound will be clearly separated from the sound uttered. The velocity of sound being, at our ordinary temperature, about 340 metres per second, the tenth of this is 34 metres. But experiment shows that about five syllables are pronounced in one second, therefore the time necessary to pronounce one syllable is one-fifth of a

second. In this time sound passes over twice 34, or 68 metres.

It follows that, if the reflecting wall be at a distance of 34 metres from the observer, one syllable when pronounced would take one-tenth of a second to be transmitted to the wall, and another tenth of a second to return to the observer; in all, therefore, one-fifth of a second. Therefore the echo would reach the ear of the observer after the syllable had been pronounced, and therefore separate and distinct. In this case the echo is called *monosyllabic;* it is called *dissyllabic* when two syllables can reach the observer distinctly. This happens when the wall is at twice the distance—that is to say, at a distance of about 68 metres. At a triple distance an echo may be trisyllabic, and so on. An echo may also be multiple, when the sound is reflected from two parallel walls, placed at a sufficient distance from each other. The most interesting case of this sort is certainly that of *Simonetta,* near Milan, a villa with two lateral wings. The report of a pistol is repeated as often as thirty-two times.

Examples of echoes are found almost everywhere. Their explanation is always easy; it seems therefore useless to dwell longer on the point.

CHAPTER III.

1. Characteristics of sound, and difference between musical sound and noise—2. Loudness of sound, and the various causes on which it depends—3. Principle of the superposition of sounds—4. Sounding-boards and resonators.

1. All the different musical sounds in nature, whatever may be their origin, and by whatever means they may be propagated, may be distinguished from each other by three different qualities.

Firstly, By the greater or less energy by which they are produced, or by their *loudness*.

Secondly, By their *pitch*.

Thirdly, By a certain characteristic difference, by which even an almost unpractised ear easily distinguishes the sound of the violin from that of the flute, that of the pianoforte from that of the human voice, &c., even though these sounds are all of the same loudness and the same pitch. This characteristic difference is called "quality," "tone," or "*timbre.*"

We ought, then, to examine on what these three different characteristics of sound depend. But before entering into this important matter, it is necessary to explain what is really meant by *sound*, when its qualities are spoken of.

A distinction is generally made in physics between *sound* and *noise*. Sound is the result of very regular vibrations which follow a law, complicated perhaps, but still a law. When the vibrations assume the simplest possible form—viz., that offered by the oscillations of the pendulum—the resulting sound is called *simple*, or a simple note; if the law be more complex, the sound is called *compound*, or a compound note. Noise, on the contrary, is a mixture of sounds collected together under no law, or under some law so complicated that the ear neither understands nor feels it. It follows that in most cases it is easy to distinguish the one from the other, but the limit between sound and noise is not always so clearly drawn. That which is a sound to one, is a noise to another, and *vice versâ*. The confused sound produced by the movement of the waves of the sea is generally considered to be a noise; but an attentive and practised ear distinguishes determinate musical sounds, and finds a musical meaning. Thus the poets speak often, and not without reason, of the harmony of the waves. An orchestra, when the individual instrumentalists are tuning their instruments and preparing to play, produces a noise which may perhaps be considered as the line of demarcation between musical sound and noise. In fact, there really is a considerable amount of music in it, although perhaps somewhat irregular, and the general impression produced is by no means disagreeable.

A fine or practised ear is able to pick out a determinate note from the midst of a confused noise. Often those who have not the habit are not aware of the presence of a more marked note in the midst of so many others; but with very little attention it becomes easy to recognise it.

In order to demonstrate this fact, use is made of a series of eight small boards, which are all of the same length and breadth, and which differ only in thickness. If one of these boards be allowed to fall on a bench, most people would be unable to distinguish any note in the noise of the blow. But a very marked note is there. To make it, however, perfectly evident, the eight boards may be allowed to fall one after another. They are tuned so as to produce the musical scale, which will be perceived very distinctly. It follows that in the confused noise, produced by the fall of each board, there is a note, which at first is not easily perceived, but which is nevertheless sufficiently clear and distinct.

In the study which we have now commenced, I shall always consider musical sounds, or notes, and not noises, because the attempt to determine the quality of a noise would be meaningless. It has no definite pitch, loudness, or *timbre.*

2. This being so, let us now investigate what may be the causes on which the modification of the loudness of musical sounds depends, or by which it is produced. The loudness depends, in the first place, on the greater or less energy by which the sound is produced. Now, all the experiments described in the earlier part of this work show that greater energy produces a more marked vibra-

tory movement in the particles of the sonorous body, in the sense that each vibrating particle traverses a longer space. The law of isochronism of vibrations shows that the duration is independent of the space passed over, within a certain approximation, which is generally considered sufficient. We will call the greatest space passed over by each particle the *amplitude* of its vibration, therefore we may say that the greater or less energy by which a sound is produced only influences the amplitude of the vibrations, and not their duration. In other words, *the loudness of a sound is represented by the amplitude of the vibrations causing it.*

The loudness of a sound depends also on the nature and density of the body which is to transmit it. In fact, a sounding body is heard in different degrees of loudness, according as the sound is transmitted by air, some other gas, water, or some other liquid or solid body. As to the density, it is enough for me to refer to the experiment described in the second chapter, of a bell under a glass receiver. When the air is completely exhausted, the sound can scarcely be heard, and the sound becomes stronger and stronger as the air is gradually allowed to enter the receiver. The loudness depends, again, on the distance of the sounding body. It is a general law of nature, confirmed by numerous experiments and by theory, that all those phenomena, whatever they may be, which have the property of being transmitted equally in all directions, must follow the inverse ratio of the square of the distance.

Sound belongs to precisely this class of phenomena—in fact, under like conditions, it is transmitted equally in every direction. It follows that its loudness must vary inversely as the square of the distance; which means that a sound that has a given loudness at a certain distance is found at double the distance to have a loudness four times less—in other words, its loudness is reduced to one-fourth. At three times the distance the loudness would be one-ninth, and for a distance twenty times greater, the loudness would be $\frac{1}{400}$ of the original loudness.

3. The loudness depends, again, on the presence of other bodies, capable of vibrating together with the principal body. We have already seen that sound is stronger in an enclosed place than in an open one. This arises from the multiple reflection in the interior of the place, by which the vibrations which exist within it are not able to disperse, and therefore come in greater number to the ear of the observer. This is only a particular case, treating rather of the conservation of existing vibrations than of the creation of new ones.

But experiment shows that whenever a body vibrates, other bodies placed near it are able to enter into a state of vibration, on this condition only, *that such bodies shall be capable by themselves of producing the same note.* This interesting fact, which deserves a moment's consideration, may be demonstrated in many ways.

Take a sonometer on which two equal strings are stretched, tuned to give the same note. In order to show whether they are in a state of vibration in any given case or no, place paper riders on the two strings, as described in the first chapter [5]. If one of the two strings be rubbed with the bow so that it may give its fundamental note, all the riders placed on this string will be thrown up into the air. But it will be observed at the same time, that the other string, which has not even been touched, also exhibits the same phenomenon, although more feebly: its riders will also after a little hesitation be thrown off.

If the riders be replaced on the two strings, and one of the strings be touched at its middle point and rubbed with the bow, a node is set up in the middle, and a higher note is produced. The second string begins to vibrate of its own accord in the same way; all the riders are thrown off except one, which is the one corresponding to the middle node. This means that the second string vibrates in the same way as the first.

This may be continued: the first string being made to vibrate in any way whatever, the riders on the second string will show that it immediately begins to vibrate in the same way. The vibrations of the first string are transmitted to the wooden bridge on which it rests, and thence to the second string. They are also transmitted from the first to the second string by means of the air, and the vibratory movement is the same in both strings.

But the vibratory movement of the second string no longer takes place, if it is unable by vibrating alone to give the same note as the first.

To demonstrate this, let one of the strings be stretched a little more, so that there may be a sensible difference of note between the two strings—for example, a semi-tone. The first string may then be rubbed how and to whatever extent you please, but no movement is now observed in the second. It was not therefore the purely mechanical action of the blow or shock given to the instrument which produced in the previous instance the beautiful phenomenon observed.

The following is another experiment, tending to show the same law: Take a tuning-fork, mounted, as is usual, on a wooden box. Being rubbed with a bow, it gives a very clear pure note. Now take an organ-pipe, which itself would give the same note. Scarcely is it made to sound near the tuning-fork, without, however, touching it, than the tuning-fork is heard to reproduce the same note. But the phenomenon no longer takes place, when instead of the first pipe one is used which gives a different note from that of the tuning-fork.

Two equal tuning-forks exhibit this phenomenon in a very marked manner. Even when placed at a great distance from each other, the one sounds directly the other sounds. This no longer happens if the tuning-forks do not give the same note. A convincing proof of this may be obtained by taking two different tuning-forks, or even by slightly altering the note of one of the two former tuning-forks by fastening, by means of some wax, a small coin to one of its branches. It will not now sound.

The following is a third method of demonstrating the same law (fig. 19): Take a cylindrical glass jar *a*, and

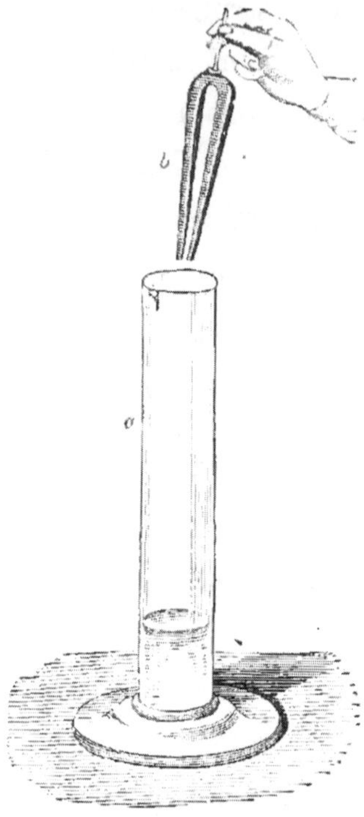

Fig. 19.

make a tuning-fork *b* vibrate over it. The sound of the tuning-fork is not in the least reinforced. By pouring water into the jar, however, the volume of the air enclosed in it is gradually diminished. By pouring in more and more, a point is arrived at where the sound is considerably reinforced. If more be poured in, the phenomenon ceases. The quantity of water which must be put into the jar in order to obtain the greatest possible reinforcement, can thus be determined by a few trials. This point being found, let us next look for the cause of this reinforcement of the sound.

Take the jar and blow gently across the upper edge; a feeble note is produced by the vibration of the air, like that of an organ-pipe, and this note is exactly that of the tuning-fork. If, on the other hand, the water be poured away, or more be added, notes may be obtained by blowing in the same manner, but they are no longer the same as the note given by the tuning-fork.

The same conclusion is arrived at by means of *Savart's bell* (fig. 20). A large bell *a* when rubbed by a bow pro-

Fig. 20.

duces a powerful note. A hollow cylinder of wood, with a movable bottom *b*, is so constructed that it can be brought near it. By altering the position of the movable bottom, and thus modifying the internal dimensions of the cylinder (the open end of which is turned towards the bell), the point at which the reinforcement of the sound is greatest is easily found. The effect obtained is considerable when the cylinder is brought near.

When the sound of the bell is still strong, the reinforcement produced by the cylinder is very sensible. The effect is still more remarkable when the sound of the bell is allowed to diminish so that it can scarcely be heard; on bringing the cylinder nearer, it becomes very marked.

4. These experiments demonstrate, then, that the reinforcement of a sound only takes place when there are

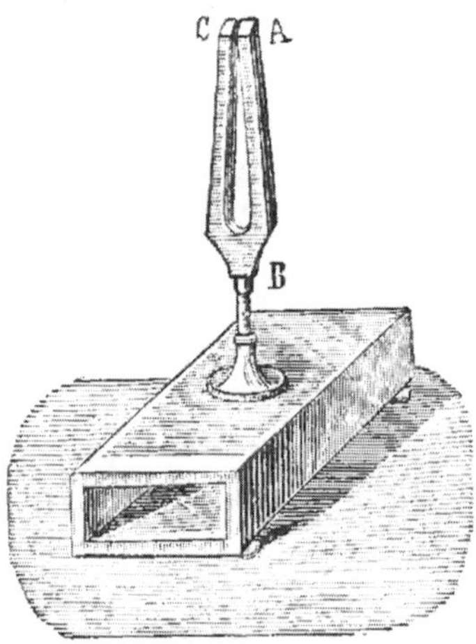

Fig. 21.

other bodies in the neighbourhood of the sounding body themselves capable of giving the same note. This important law of resonance has been applied to many cases. The sounding-board is founded on this law. In fact, tuning-forks give a very feeble sound by themselves. They are therefore often mounted on wooden boxes, as in fig. 21, where the tuning-fork AC is attached to the box that supports it by means of the foot B.

The boxes have different dimensions, according to the dimensions of their tuning-forks, and enclose a quantity of air determined for each note. They considerably reinforce the sound of the tuning-fork, provided that their dimensions have been well chosen.

An interesting form of sounding-board, which has acquired a great importance of late years, is that called *Helmholtz's resonator.* These resonators are hollow metallic spheres or even cylinders of different sizes, furnished with two apertures. One *a*, the larger, only serves to maintain a communication between the external air and that in the sphere; the other *b*, the smaller, has the form of an orifice with an elongated neck, and is intended to be inserted in the ear [figs. 22 and 23].

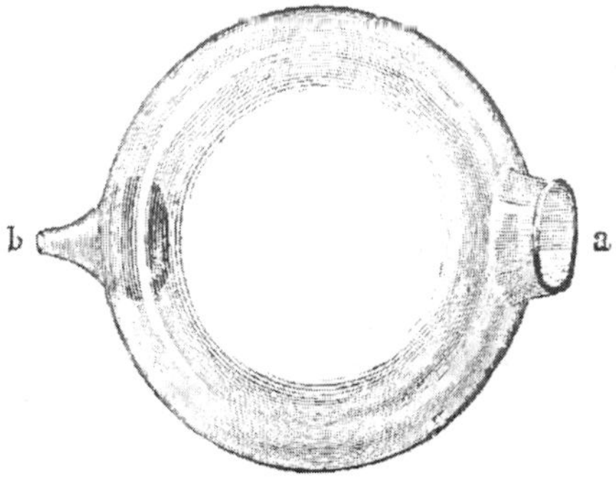

Fig. 22.

For use, it is necessary to have a series of these resonators of different sizes. Each of them, according to the volume of air that it contains, reinforces one single note;

the larger ones serve for the low, the smaller for the high notes.

The spherical resonators are really the best, and give the clearest phenomena. Nevertheless, a cylindrical and

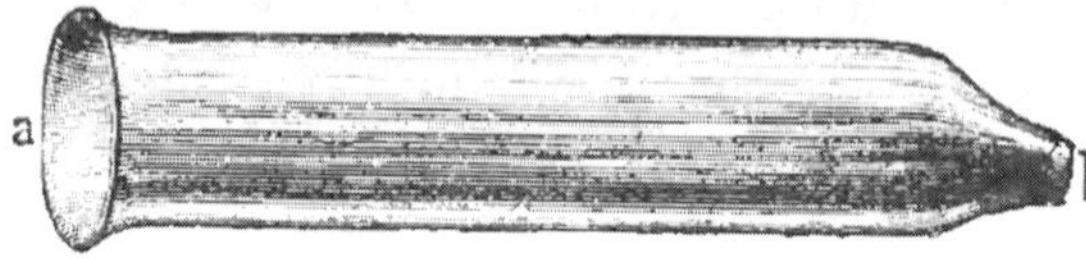

Fig. 23.

even conical form is sometimes adopted, because they are more readily held in the hand, and are therefore more convenient to manage.

It is easy to show that these resonators reinforce musical sounds, and each one only one particular note. If a series of tuning-forks, which give notes corresponding to those of the resonators, be taken, the sound of each fork is reinforced by its corresponding resonator. This effect may be still better observed if the point of the resonator be introduced into one ear and the other be closed with the hand.

It is to be noticed that no resonator will produce this effect unless it be combined with its corresponding tuning-fork.

Let us suppose that there are a number of notes mixed together, our ears then separate them with difficulty. But if an observer wishes to know whether amongst all these there is some one particular note, he need only take the corresponding resonator and hold it to his ear. If the note in question is there, it will be reinforced, and thus he will easily be able to distinguish it amongst all the others.

An example of this kind is easily to be found. If a number of suitable tuning-forks be sounded together, a very agreeable harmony will be produced, in which, however, an unpractised ear would not perhaps be able to distinguish the individual notes composing it. By means of resonators it is quite easy to do so. To take another example, the human voice is very rich in notes, and even when merely speaking, we modulate the voice much more than is generally believed. If a resonator be taken and held to the ear while the observer speaks in his natural voice, every now and then he will distinctly perceive in the resonator the note to which it corresponds, which signifies that amongst the many notes which he uses in speaking, there is the particular one to which the resonator corresponds. He could thus with a little patience analyse successively all the notes used by a person whilst speaking.

In a later chapter, following the example of *Helmholtz*, I will show what use can be made of the employment of these resonators. I will show [chapter ix.] how one of the most important and most delicate laws may be observed and followed by this means.

The case of resonators and of the sounding-boards described above must not be confounded with that of the sounding-boards forming part of certain musical instruments. The sonometer, which has been described in an earlier chapter, the violin and other stringed instruments, the pianoforte, &c., have sounding-boards intended to reinforce not only one note alone, but all the notes in turn, and as far as possible to a uniform extent. It would be a very bad musical instrument in which the different notes had not the same loudness, when the method of producing them is the same. The theory of these sounding-boards is much more complicated, and is not easy to follow. I will confine myself to saying, that in order to obtain this effect it is necessary that the sounding-board be relatively very large, and that it should have a particular shape determined by experience. In this case the sounding-board corresponds to a very low note, and is subject, like a vibrating string, to such laws that it corresponds not only to the lower note, but also to many successively higher notes.

If the lowest note be very low, it can reinforce so many notes that their number may be considered infinite.

This takes place especially in the case of plates, membranes, and large vibrating boards, and practice shows that all that is wanted in the way of reinforcing notes can be obtained.

CHAPTER IV.

1. Measure of the number of vibrations; the graphic method—2. Cagniard de la Tour's Siren—3. Pitch of sounds; limit of audible sounds, of musical sounds and of the human voice—4. The "normal pitch"—5. Laws of the vibrations of a string, and of harmonics.

1. The second characteristic quality of musical sounds is their *pitch*. Every ear, however little practised, distinguishes a high note from a low one, even when the interval is not large. I propose to demonstrate *that the pitch depends on the number of vibrations that a sounding body makes in each second of time*, in such a way that the low notes are characterised by the small number, the high notes by the large number of their vibrations per second.

In order to solve this problem, we must first solve another: how the number of vibrations is to be determined? There are many methods in physics used for this purpose.

One method I have already to a great extent indicated—the graphic method, by means of which the vibrations of a tuning-fork were traced in the first chapter. In that experiment use was made of a cylinder, turned by hand. Naturally the motion could not be very regular, but if instead of the hand, use is made of one of the many mechanical equivalents, a perfectly regular motion can easily be obtained; and further, the velocity of this motion may be determined. Suppose, for example, that the cylinder has a velocity of one turn per second; the tuning-fork will then record its vibrations, and to know their number per second we have only to count how many there are in one complete turn of the cylinder. The calculation is equally simple if the cylinder makes any other number of turns in a second. If, for example, the cylinder only makes five, we have only to count the vibrations in five turns, and the determination will be accurate, if the number of turns that the cylinder makes per second is accurately determined. This is often possible, and I will describe later on a very simple *counter*, by which the number of turns of a rotating apparatus is measured. The problem may then be solved by this means, as far as the vibrations of a tuning-fork are concerned.

2. At this point it becomes necessary to make the reader acquainted with another instrument, which answers this purpose to perfection, and which offers the advantage over the turning cylinder of not requiring for its use a slight change of the note, for a point has to be attached to the vibrating tuning-fork to trace its vibrations. This instrument is *Cagniard de la Tour's Siren.* Figs. 24, 25, and 26 show the arrangement of the instrument. It consists of a hollow empty cylindrical box BBB, which by means of its neck can be put in communication with a blower capable of

furnishing a constant current of air. In the upper end of the cylinder are a certain number of equidistant holes, disposed on the periphery of a circle concentric to the outline of the rim itself. These holes are all oblique, so

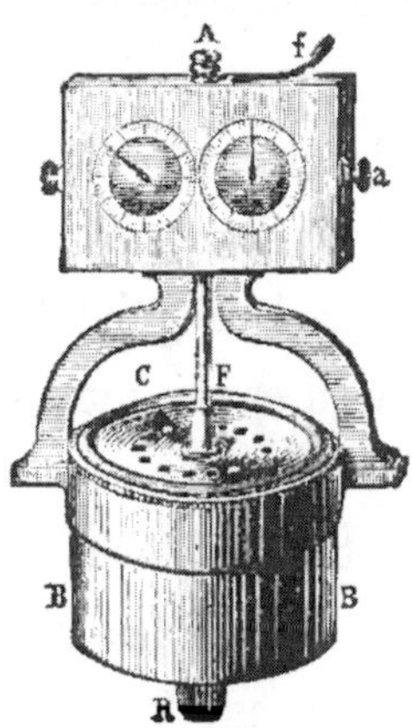

Fig. 24.

Fig. 25.

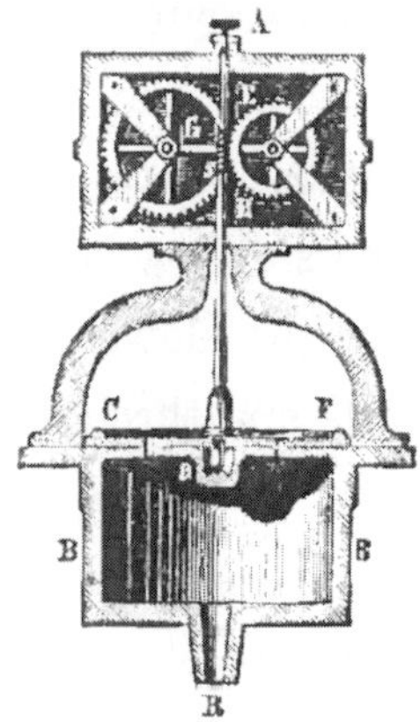

Fig. 26.

as to form an angle of about 45° with the vertical line. Over these holes is a metal disc C, which covers them entirely, and which is able to turn rapidly on a vertical axis A. This disc carries an equal number of holes, corresponding exactly in position and size with the holes in the disc below. These holes are also oblique, but in a different direction, and form an angle of about 45° with the vertical, but an angle of 90° with the direction of the holes beneath. Fig. 25 shows the section of the two discs, the fixed one and the movable one, as well as the arrangement of the holes. The holes *p* slope in one direction and the holes *p'* in the other. Fig. 26 is a drawing in section of the whole apparatus, in which is shown the hollow cylindrical box B of the siren, the movable disc CF, and the axis Aa on which it turns. When a current of air is forced into the cylinder by means of the blower, this current passes, it is true, through the holes; but on account of their obliquity, it strikes against their sides. The movable disc thus receives a series of impulses, all in the sáme direction, and therefore begins to turn. It turns quickly when the current is strong, and slowly when the current is weak; by suitably controlling the blower, the force of the current can be regulated at will, and through it the velocity of rotation of the movable disc.

But the current of air that enters the cylinder in a regular jet, can only pass out through the holes intermittently as soon as the movable disc has begun to turn. The reason for this is very simple. The air only passes out at the moments when the holes in the movable disc coincide with the holes in the fixed disc; it is, on the other hand, intercepted when the holes in the movable disc are over the unperforated parts between the holes in the fixed disc. It follows that the air must come out of the siren in the form of little puffs, which will be more frequent as the number of holes in the two discs is greater, and the velocity of rotation of the movable disc is greater. Suppose, for example, that each disc has twenty-five holes, as is the case in the siren I am now describing [twelve are shown in the drawing, but the number is arbitrary]. Suppose further that the velocity of rotation is one turn per second of time. In this case each hole in the upper disc will give out twenty-five puffs of air in a second of time. If, however, the movable disc makes 2, 3, 4, &c., turns in a second, I must multiply the number of holes —*i.e.*, 25—by 2, 3, 4, &c., or generally by the number of turns, to find the number of puffs of air produced by each hole per second.

When the siren is set in action, a very pure note is formed, low at first when the disc turns slowly, but higher as the velocity of the disc increases. The note is produced because the external air over the instrument is struck regularly by the puffs of air from the siren. These periodical blows produce vibrations in the external air, the number of which per second evidently corresponds to the number of blows received per second. We can therefore produce at will, by controlling the blower, any note we please, be it high or low; we can at the same time calculate the number of vibrations per second corresponding to it, as there is a means of determining the number of turns that the instrument makes in a second of time.

The very simple counter, which is placed at the top of the instrument, and which is represented in fig. 26, answers this purpose. To the movable disc CF is fixed a vertical steel arbor A*a*, which carries at its upper end a few turns S of what is called *an endless screw.* The teeth of a toothed wheel EH gear into this screw, so that it moves forward one tooth for one turn of the arbor and movable disc. To the axis of the toothed wheel is fastened a hand, like that of a clock [see fig. 24]; a graduated circle enables its movements, and by its means those of the toothed wheel, to be observed. Each division on the circle corresponds to one tooth of the wheel, or one revolution of the movable disc of the siren. The toothed wheel has 100 teeth, therefore the divisions under the hand are hundredth parts, arranged round an internal periphery. A second toothed wheel, with a second hand and a second set of divisions, is so arranged that for each revolution of the first wheel it moves forward one tooth and its hand one division. Its divisions show, therefore, each hundred turns, whilst those of the first show the single turns of the movable disc of the siren.

This system enables us easily to determine the number of turns made by the siren in a given time, even though it may be very high.

To facilitate the counting, the toothed wheel can be brought near to the main arbor and moved away from it at will by means of the button *a* (fig. 24), which allows of a small displacement; the wheel is thus put in action for as long as may be desired, and may be stopped at will.

The instrument is thus used. Suppose we wish to determine the number of vibrations per second which corresponds to the note of a tuning-fork. We have:—

(1.) To reproduce with the siren the same note in such a way as to keep it constant for a certain length of time.

(2.) This being obtained, to set in action a stop-watch and the counter of the siren, and thus to determine the number of turns per second.

These two operations are easily performed. The first result is obtained by suitably loading the blower. The note of the siren is at first very low, then rises slowly, and after some time remains constant. The reason of this constancy is this, that the current of air is just able to overcome the friction of the instrument for this given velocity. But say the note of the tuning-fork is higher: then in order to get up to it, the blower must be loaded more. The note rises suddenly, and after a few trials the weight is found which must be put on the blower in order to reproduce the note of the tuning-fork and keep it steady. The note keeps constant for a certain length of time, during which the second operation can be easily completed. This being arranged, the exact position of the pointers is observed, the stop-watch is set going, and so afterwards, at a chosen moment, is the counter of the siren, which is left in action for ten seconds. It is always better to operate for a somewhat long time rather than for one second only, because in the former case a small error committed in setting the counter going is less felt than in the latter.

When the ten seconds have elapsed, the action of the counter is stopped, and from the position of the pointers the number of turns made by the instrument in ten seconds is seen.

In this case say there are 358 turns in ten seconds—

that is to say, that 35·8 turns correspond to one second. To know now the number of vibrations per second, since the disc of the siren has 25 holes, 35·8 must be multiplied by 25, which gives 895 as the number of vibrations per second. The tuning-fork in question, therefore, produces a note of 895 vibrations per second of time. As we have operated in this case, so we can operate in any other case whatsoever. The siren lends itself admirably to researches of this nature. It only requires a practised ear to be able to reproduce exactly a particular note. Whether we wish to have recourse to the graphic method, or whether we wish to make use of the siren, we have acquired the power of determining the number of vibrations of very many, or, I might say, of all notes.

3. Let us now consider the more important results which have been arrived at on this point, by a minute and accurate examination of the facts.

What is the limit of audible sounds? Does our ear perceive, as a note, any number of vibrations whatever, or is our perception confined between certain limits? That there is a lower limit may easily be demonstrated by means of the siren. When the siren is set in action, and at first turns very slowly, the single puffs of air are heard singly, but no note is perceived. A very low note, however, begins when the siren turns a little faster. By more exact experiments it is found that there must be at least sixteen vibrations in a second of time in order to produce a note; and this limit is only reached by using a very powerful instrument—that is to say, an instrument able to give a somewhat loud note. In other cases—as, for instance, in the case of the common siren—twenty or twenty-five vibrations must take place per second, in order to produce an appreciable note.

It is more difficult to fix a high limit for sound. If the blower be successively loaded, the siren turns faster and faster, the note grows sharper and sharper, and at last becomes shrill and disagreeable. But with an ordinary siren it would not be possible to obtain a velocity above a certain limit, because the friction would prevent a very high velocity. To solve the problem, *Despretz* made use of smaller and smaller tuning-forks, and finally succeeded in demonstrating that there is an upper limit for sound, beyond which our ear perceives nothing.

This limit was fixed by him at very nearly 38,000 vibrations in a second, a figure that has been finally confirmed by Helmholtz; but it is probable that it differs in different individuals. We may conclude that sonorous vibrations lie between the limits 16 and 38,000 per second.

But all the notes comprised between these extreme limits are not musical notes, properly so called—that is to say, notes advantage of which is taken in practical music. The notes that are too low are badly heard; those that are too high are unpleasant.

In the modern pianoforte of seven complete octaves, the base A corresponds to about 27½, the highest A to 3480 vibrations per second. Therefore, taking into account the differences of tuning, it may be said that the notes of the pianoforte range from 27 to 3500 vibrations per second.

In the violin, the fourth open string [the lowest note] corresponds to about 193 vibrations; the highest note may be fixed at about 3500.

This number is not, however, the highest. Some pianofortes go up to the seventh C, which corresponds to about 4200; and with the piccolo 4700 and more vibrations per second are reached. But the real gain that music has realised from so great an extension is very doubtful. Notes that are too high are shrill, and lose entirely that full, sweet quality which constitutes the principal characteristic of musical notes. It may be concluded, without exaggeration, that musical notes are comprised between 27 and 4000 vibrations per second.

The question of the human voice, and of the limits between which it acts, is also interesting. In considering it, we must distinguish between the voice of men and of women. The latter is represented by about twice as many vibrations per second as that of men. Subdivisions are made for musical purposes in each of these classes of voice: thus there are, for men, bass, baritone, and tenor voices; for women, contralto, mezzo-soprano, and soprano voices. The following table shows the limits of each of these voices for a normal case, as they may reasonably be expected from a good and practised singer. The figures written in brackets represent cases of exceptional voices which the stage has produced up to the present time:—

Extent and Limits of the Human Voice.

Bass . . .	[B = 61]	E = 82	. .	D = 293	[F = 348]
Baritone . .	(D = 73)	F = 87	. .	F♯ = 370	[G = 392]
Tenor . . .	(G = 98)	A = 109	. .	A = 435	(C♯ = 544)*
Contralto . .	(C = 110)	E = 164	. .	F = 696	(A = 870)
Mezzo-soprano	(E = 164)	F = 174	. .	A = 870	(B = 976)
Soprano . .	(G = 196)	A = 218	. .	C = 1044	(E = 1305)

The well-developed voice of a single singer embraces about two octaves; in the case of women a little more. The extreme limits of the human voice [man's and woman's combined] may be fixed within four octaves, from C = 65 up to C = 1044, certain extreme cases not included.†

4. A question of some practical importance has latterly been raised and solved: that of establishing a uniform pitch for all countries, so as to make it possible to tune instruments uniformly. For the purpose of tuning musical instruments, a small tuning-fork is generally used, which gives the A which corresponds to the second open string of the violin, and is in a seven-octave pianoforte the fifth A, counting from the lowest note. All the

* Tamberlik's overpraised C♯.

† Certain marvellously gifted voices have had more extended limits; the voices of Cruvelli, Catalani, Patti, and Nilsson will always be celebrated for this. The highest voice seems to be that of *Bastardella*, whom Mozart heard at Parma in 1770, which had three and a half octaves, and went up almost to 2000 vibrations. Also the voice of eunuchs, and especially that of the celebrated *Farinelli*, have a very great range.

different theatres of Italy and Europe have adopted pitches differing from each other; and even in the same theatre the A goes on gradually rising. At Paris, in 1700, it was 405; later on, 425; in 1855, 440; and in 1857, 448 vibrations per second. This last number has since remained steady at the Berlin Theatre; but the pitch of the Scala at Milan corresponds to 451½, and that of Covent Garden Theatre at London to 455 vibrations per second.

This state of things was very unpleasant to singers, for whom it was no easy matter to satisfy requirements differing so sensibly in different countries, especially when it is remembered that modern music, to increase the effect, is written very much on the extreme notes, and especially on the high ones, and therefore makes a great call upon the singers. To this may be added the tendency of the manufacturers of musical instruments, and especially of brass instruments, to raise the pitch continually, in order to give a greater brilliancy of tone to their instruments.

As may be seen from the example given of the rise of pitch at Paris, it thus came about that from the last century until now the pitch had been rising considerably everywhere, and had a tendency to rise still higher. It was therefore necessary to find a remedy for so grave an inconvenience, and an international commission fixed as the *normal pitch* (usually called the *diapason normal*) a tuning-fork giving 435 vibrations per second of time.

5. I will close this chapter by demonstrating an important law, at which we arrive by studying the number of the vibrations per second of a string. When the whole string vibrates in one vibration, it gives its lowest note, which I have called the fundamental note. If the string be divided, by touching it with the finger or a feather, into two, three, four, &c., parts, higher and higher notes are obtained, which form that which is called *an harmonic series.* The notes of this harmonic series are not notes taken at random. They are very agreeable to the ear in relation to the fundamental note, and have great importance, as we shall see in the sequel, in the theory of music and of musical instruments. It may be asked, then, if there is a simple law to regulate these notes, as the method of their production is so simple.

To answer this question, all that is needed is to determine the number of vibrations of the string for the fundamental note, and for the successive harmonic notes.

Carefully repeated experiments show that simple relations exist between all these notes. Let us suppose, for example, that the fundamental note makes 128 vibrations per second; the second harmonic, which is obtained by dividing the string into two parts, then makes twice 128 vibrations, or 256 per second; the third harmonic, which is obtained by dividing the string into three parts, makes three times 128, or 384 vibrations per second; the fourth harmonic, which arises from the division of the string into four parts, makes four times 128, or 512 vibrations per second, and so on. Therefore, calling the fundamental note 1, the harmonic notes will be exactly represented, in respect of their vibrations per second, by the whole numbers, 2, 3, 4, &c. By considering the mode of formation of these notes, the following two laws are arrived at:—

(1.) The harmonics increase, in respect of the number of their vibrations per second, as the whole numbers.

(2.) The number of vibrations per second of a string always varies inversely as its length.

This second law holds for all cases, even when a string is shortened in any manner whatever; on the sonometer this shortening is accomplished in a very simple manner. Besides the two fixed bridges on which the string rests, there is a third movable bridge, by means of which the string can be shortened at will. A scale of centimetres and millimetres allows the length of the effective part of the string to be measured in any case. A sonometer constructed in this manner affords the simplest and shortest means of determining the number of vibrations of a note. The operation is performed as follows: The string of the sonometer is stretched so that when vibrating in its whole length (one metre), it gives a known, constant note—for example, one of 128 vibrations per second. When the string is thus tuned, the sonometer is ready for immediate use. If it be desired to know the number of vibrations of a given musical sound, that note is exactly reproduced by sliding the bridge along, and so shortening the string; the scale under the string gives its new length. Let this be, for example, 432 millimetres; then, as the number of vibrations varies inversely as the length of the string, we arrive at the following proportion:—

$$432 : 1000 :: 128 : x$$

$$\text{Whence} \quad x = \frac{128 \times 1000}{432} = 296$$

Therefore the note makes 296 vibrations per second.

This method of determining the number of the vibrations is the simplest of all. It is capable of giving results of sufficient accuracy, and may be adopted directly the laws of the vibrations of strings have been established.

CHAPTER V.

1. Musical sounds—2. Law of simple ratio—3. Unison, interference—4. Beats—5. Their explanation—6. Resultant notes—7. Octaves and other harmonics—8. Consonant chords and their limits—9. The major fifth, fourth, sixth, and third; the minor third and sixth—10. The seventh harmonic.

1. It has been shown in the last chapter that all the sounds in nature are not musical sounds, properly so called. In order that a sound may acquire a musical character, it must satisfy the essential condition of being agreeable to the ear. It is on this account that all the sounds produced by imperfect instruments must be rejected, whatever may be their pitch. All those, also, which are too high or too low must be rejected as either disagreeable or insignificant. There remain, therefore, the notes comprised between about 27 and 4000 vibrations per second, which form an interval of a little more than seven octaves, between which limits the music of all countries and all nations is written.

But it would be a grave error to suppose that between the limits hinted at, all the notes can be used arbitrarily or at hazard. Experience shows that any one of these notes may be chosen in executing or beginning a piece of music. But when once this note is selected, all the others that are to follow or accompany it are limited, and we move in a very restricted circle. This is not only the case in our modern music, but also holds good for the music of every epoch. There is no instance known of a musical system, however barbarous it may be, in which the choice of the notes is left to the fancy of the composer or performer. The history of music, on the contrary, teaches us that it has always been sought to select, from the enormous number of possible notes, an infinitely more restricted number, according to certain established rules, in which musical instinct was at times influenced by scientific theories of greater or less value, giving the preference to one and sometimes to another of such theories. We will consider later on the different conceptions which instinctively or rationally have guided different nations in the historical development of music. For the present I will content myself by saying that in our modern music, art has outstripped science with rapid strides, and it is only quite recently that the latter has been able to give a complete and rational explanation of what the former has effected by means of delicate æsthetic feeling.

2. It may be established as one of the fundamental principles of our music, that the ear can only endure notes, be they simultaneous or successive, on this condition—namely, *that they should bear simple ratios to each other in respect of the number of their vibrations per second;*

that is to say, that the ratio of the number of vibrations per second of the notes should be expressed by low numbers. All the bearings of this simple principle will be pointed out in a later chapter, and since, thanks to the great researches of *Helmholtz*, it has acquired of late years, notwithstanding its simplicity, an even simpler and wider significance, I will for the present content myself with indicating its more important consequences.

It is not without some hesitation that I enter upon such a subject. I shall have to go through a series of figures, and indeed to argue entirely upon figures. The road is rather a rough and thorny one, but I trust that, like the traveller who courageously climbs the steep and rugged sides of a mountain in order to enjoy at last a vast and magnificent panorama, so from the highest peak of this argument a vast horizon will open out before the reader, in which he will discover the synthesis of one of the grandest creations of the imagination—a creation that in itself forms one of the most brilliant pages in the history of human culture.

3. The most simple ratio that can be imagined between the vibrations per second of two notes is that in which both are represented by the same number of vibrations. The two notes are then said to be *in unison.* If they be sounded one after the other, they only form one more prolonged note; if they be sounded together, they only give one note of double loudness. It sometimes happens, however, that two equal notes, instead of supporting each

other, are enfeebled in their effects. Cases of this kind are due to what is called *interference.* This happens whenever the vibrations of the two notes are made in the reverse way—that is to say, when the vibrating body of the first note makes a movement in one given direction, whilst the other makes a precisely contrary movement. It is evident that such opposing vibratory movements must destroy each other's effect, when superposed in the air in which they are propagated; as a particle of air which ought to move at the same time and with the same force in two opposite directions, not being able to follow either, remains at rest.

Fig. 27.

The apparatus represented in fig. 27 enables us to produce interference at will. It is composed of a vibrating plate in which a Chladni's figure is formed by the vibrating segments A B, A′ B′. The vibrations in two contiguous segments, as A′ and B′, are contrary, or reverse, inasmuch as when the particles at A′ fall, those at B′ rise, and *vice versa;* they are similar in two opposite segments, as at A and A′. DCE is a bifurcated pipe which gives by itself the same note as the plate, and is closed at the top by a paper membrane, which serves, when sprinkled with sand, to indicate the vibrations in the pipe. If now the plate be caused to vibrate, and some sand be sprinkled on it to indicate its mode of vibration, two points having similar vibrations, as A and A′, may be selected, and the branches of the pipe placed over them, without, however, allowing them to touch; the sand on the membrane will then dance about and dispose itself regularly, which shows that the air in the pipe vibrates, because the vibrations of A and A′ support each other in producing this effect. Again, two points having an opposite motion, as A′ and B′, may be selected and the branches of the pipe placed over them; the effect will then be nil, and the sand will not move.

From all this we may conclude that *when two equal and simultaneous vibratory movements are superimposed, they support each other, but that, on the other hand, their effect is destroyed if they are equal and opposite.*

4. The question is interesting as to what happens when the two notes produced are almost though not quite identical, and have not therefore quite the same number of vibrations per second. A new phenomenon then appears, known by the name of *beats.*

In order to show what these beats really are, the following experiment may be adopted. Two large equal organ-pipes are taken which give two low, strong, identical notes. These being attached to a blower, and sounded together, we obtain the same note, only of double loudness, which is obtained by sounding either pipe without the other. But the pipes are so made that it is easy slightly to alter the note of either. For this purpose there is an aperture in the upper part of one of the walls of each pipe closed by a movable plate, by lowering which more or less the aperture in the pipe can be opened to a greater or less extent; the effect thus produced is similar to that obtained by shortening the pipe. The note is slightly raised, and by means of the movable plate it can be regulated at will.

Now let the note of one of the two pipes be slightly raised. The difference between the notes of the two pipes is so small that even a practised ear can scarcely perceive it for such low notes. But if the two pipes be sounded together, a sound is obtained of varying loudness, now strong and now feeble, and very marked jerks or shocks are perceived. These shocks are the beats. If the difference between the notes of the two pipes be very small, the beats will be very slow, not more perhaps than one in the second; but if, on the other hand, the difference be increased by raising the note of the first pipe, they will become more frequent. By suitably regulating the note of one of the pipes by means of the movable plate, and leaving the other untouched, 2, 3, 4, 5, or 10 beats per second may be obtained. In the last case, however, it is difficult to count them; but they are distinctly audible, and remain so up to 20 or even 25 per second, beyond that the ear is no longer able to distinguish them.

Beats of this kind are very common. They are more especially heard in instruments with fixed strong notes, as, for example, in the organ. They are a sure sign that the instrument is not well tuned, and afford a very simple and correct method of bringing two slightly differing notes into unison. All that need be done is to tune them until the beats cease.

In the sound of bells the phenomenon of beats is very common. In fact, it is not possible to cast a large bell so that it may present at every point a perfect homogeneity and an equal density and elasticity. The bell, therefore, easily divides into two not perfectly equal parts, which by vibrating somewhat differently produce beats.

5. It is easy to understand how these beats are produced. If two notes make exactly the same number of vibrations per second, except in the special case of interference, which will not be here taken into account, the vibrations of the two bodies coincide, and a note is produced of double loudness; but if the two notes be not of exactly the same pitch, the phenomenon is more complicated. Let it be supposed, for example, that the first note makes 100 vibrations in a second, and the other 101.

If they be sounded together, the first vibrations will almost correspond with each other, their effects will be added together, and a louder note will be produced. But at the fiftieth vibration of the first, the second note will have accomplished fifty and a half vibrations. But as a vibration always has one half in which the vibrating body moves in one direction, and another half in which it moves in the opposite direction, it follows that at the fiftieth vibration of the first note, and the corresponding half vibration of the second, the movements will be contrary, and the note will therefore be sensibly deadened, or at least more or less considerably enfeebled. To the hundredth vibration of the first note corresponds the one hundred and first vibration of the second, and from this point they again reinforce each other, and so on. It is thus seen that for each difference of one vibration there must be one strengthening and one enfeebling of the note—that is to say, one beat per second. Therefore, if there be two notes, which differ by 2, 3, 4, 5, 10 vibrations per second, there will be 2, 3, 4, 5, 10 beats per second; and the number of beats, which is easily observed, gives a very exact measure of the difference between the number of vibrations per second of the two notes. This is a very safe, practical method for determinations of this sort, because it is independent, so to speak, of the ear, or, at all events, does not require a very delicate ear.

The phenomenon of beats is not only observed when

two notes are almost in unison, but even more when the two notes are to each other, in respect to their number of vibrations per second, almost, but not quite, in some other simple proportion. Let, for example, the number of their vibrations per second be as one to two, then, if the proportion is exact, there will be no beats; if, on the other hand, the proportion be not exact, the beats are at once heard. In order to show this, take two pipes giving the fundamental note and its octave, and which can be slightly altered at will. If they be perfectly tuned and sounded together, there are no beats, and the harmony is agreeable, like one clearer and fuller note; but if one of the two notes be ever so slightly altered, immediately unpleasant beats appear, which spoil the harmony. It is easy, by an analogous reasoning to the foregoing, to explain this phenomenon. It is enough, however, here to draw this conclusion, that the beats are the simplest and most sure means of observing that two notes are not so tuned that their vibrations may be represented by a simple ratio. But as simple ratio is a necessary condition in order that harmonies may be produced which shall be agreeable to the ear, it follows that the presence of beats is a sure proof that an instrument is not properly tuned.

6. In strict relation to the phenomenon of beats, and as a necessary consequence to the combination of two notes, are those notes whose discovery, made towards the middle of the last century, is generally attributed to the celebrated violinist *Tartini*, and to which the name of

resultant notes, or sometimes *difference notes*, is usually given. The theory of these notes is not easy to give. Hitherto it has been held that when the beats become very rapid, so as to be more than 16 per second, they generate on their own account a very low note, which is the resultant note. If there be two notes—one which makes 100, and the other 125 vibrations per second—they will give 25 beats a second, which will generate a note of 25 vibrations a second. There are thus three notes—the original two of 100 and 125, and the resultant note of 25 vibrations per second.

But this explanation, however simple it may appear, and however well it may correspond to the results, is open to certain serious objections on which it is impossible to dwell. The true theory of resultant notes can only be given by means of mathematical calculation.

All that need here be said is, that resultant notes are really difference notes in this sense, that the number of their vibrations per second really corresponds to the difference of the vibrations per second of the two combined notes. Thus in the example given above, when two notes are combined together, one of 100 and the other of 125 vibrations per second, a resultant note is obtained which really corresponds to 25 vibrations per second.

These resultant notes may be experimentally observed by means of two organ-pipes, one making 200 and the other 250 vibrations per second, giving a harmony; which is represented by the ratio $\frac{5}{4}$, and which, as will be seen later on, is called a *major third.* When they are sounded together, besides these two notes, a low note is very clearly heard, which corresponds to 50 vibrations per second, a number which is the fourth part of 200, or the half of the half. It will be seen later on that the half means the lower octave of a note, therefore the half of the half signifies two octaves below this same note. It follows that the resultant note which is formed ought to be the second octave below of the note of 200 vibrations a second, which with a little attention is found to be the fact.

Resultant notes are always present, whenever two different notes are combined; and there is a very simple rule for determining them: *the number of vibrations per second of the resultant note is always equal to the difference between the number of vibrations per second of the notes that are combined.* But as it is more important in the theory of sound to know the ratios of the numbers of vibrations per second of the different notes to each other than to know the absolute number of their vibrations per second, the different notes are expressed by whole numbers; such being the case, the resultant note will also be expressed by whole numbers.

In the example given above it may be said that the notes 4 and 5 have been combined, since the ratio is the same as that between 200 and 250. The resultant note is then represented by the difference 1.

The resultant notes have great importance in the theory

of music, as will be shown later on in this chapter. As they are frequently very loud, it is necessary to take them into account, and also their ratios to other notes. If, then, several notes be combined together, it is not enough to select those which by themselves will give an agreeable harmony; it is necessary further to examine the resultant notes, and to see how these will behave in relation to the combined notes.

It may be added that these resultant notes are notes that really exist. It follows from this that they can combine with each other and produce new resultant notes, which are called resultant notes of the second order. There are thus resultant notes of the third, fourth order, &c. But as these are so very feeble that even a practised ear cannot succeed in distinguishing them, in most cases it is not worth while to take them into account.

7. The next most simple ratio that can be imagined after unison is that of 1 : 2. This is the ratio called that of the *octave*. That note is called the octave of the fundamental note that makes twice the number of vibrations per second. Doubling the number of vibrations of a note means raising it to its octave above, and *vice versa*. So, too, reducing the number of vibrations per second of a note to one-half, means descending to its octave below. The octave of the octave is represented by a number of vibrations per second four times greater, the third octave by a number eight times greater; the second,

third, &c., octaves below are expressed by $\frac{1}{4}$, $\frac{1}{8}$, &c., of the vibrations per second of the fundamental note.

The harmony of the octave with the fundamental note is very consonant. When the two notes are perfectly in tune, which is recognised by the complete absence of beats, the ear does not distinguish two notes. One single, open, clear note, as it were, is heard, with a somewhat modified *timbre.*

The Greeks, who did not use harmony, properly so called, in their music, nevertheless admitted singing in octaves; which is easily understood, when it is remembered that the voices of women and boys are an octave higher than those of adult men; therefore a chorus, singing all together, must produce an accompaniment in octaves.

The resultant note produced by the combination of the notes 1 and 2 is again 1, which means, that in the harmony of the fundamental note and its octave the resultant note serves to reinforce the fundamental note.

Other simple relations are furnished by the fundamental note 1 united to one of the notes of the harmonic series 2, 3, 4, 5, &c. The note 2 represents, as has been seen, the octave; the note 3 is the twelfth, or as it may also be called, for reasons which will be seen later on, the *fifth of the octave;* the note 4 is the octave of the octave, &c.

All these notes form agreeable harmonies with the fundamental note. Their only defect, musically speaking, is that the intervals between them and the fundamental note are very great. These harmonies, however, are certainly poor, but not unpleasant, and are especially used on the violin and other stringed instruments. The fundamental character of these harmonies is, that the resultant notes arising from them also belong to the harmonic series. Thus, for example, the resultant note of 1 and 3 is 2, that of 1 and 4 is 3, and so on; and the resultant notes of the second order are found, when we come to analyse them, to strengthen the fundamental note.

8. But music would be extremely poor if it were wished to limit it to these few notes, although they are the most natural ones. Certain brass instruments, indeed, have no other notes at their disposition, as, for example, the primitive keyless trumpet; but the melodies played on such instruments are very restricted and monotonous.

Practical musicians, therefore, have been compelled to go farther into the matter, and to see if they could not find other ratios which, although more complicated than the first, would be still simple enough to be acceptable. But it naturally follows, from the principle laid down at the head of this chapter, that the less complicated the ratios, the more perfect are the harmonies. The introduction into music of more and more complicated harmonies has therefore been made slowly and gradually. This must be considered as progress in the sense that it has increased musical resources, but it is progress made at the expense of primitive purity.

Starting from this principle, let us see how far this has been done up to the present time, and how much farther we can reasonably go. What has been said is of itself sufficient apology for the opinion of those who maintain that music is not the result of absolute æsthetic principles, but that it is rather the result of successive musical education, an education which evidently primarily depends on the æsthetic aspirations of different nations, and on the state of their culture. In fact, history shows that all bold musical innovations have had to contend with immense opposition, and it is convenient, though not consistent with truth, to look upon such resistance as only rancour or personal envy. The true reason is, that there is no mathematical expression by which to define with certainty when a ratio is simple and when not; and it is equally difficult to establish when a sound ceases to be agreeable. Whether it be more or less simple, more or less complicated, more or less agreeable, it depends on the habit of the ear how far it will follow a bold innovation. In truth, certain harmonies, which are now considered perfectly admissible, were not so considered in past centuries, especially in the early stages of music.

9. The jump from the fundamental note 1 to its octave 2 is very great, and leads to the inquiry, whether it be not possible to introduce other notes in this interval. The study of the harmonic series here offers a good precedent. In fact we have seen that the ratios 1 : 2, 1 : 3, 1 : 4, &c., are consonant. It may then be asked, if the ratios

which result from taking another note of the harmonic series as a point of departure—such as 2 : 3, 2 : 4, 3 : 4 —are not also consonant; which signifies, in other terms, that the notes of the harmonic series are consonant not only with the fundamental note, but also with each other.

This question may be approached in a different way. Given that the interval between 1 and 2 can or ought to be filled up with other notes, it may be asked, what will be the notes which will present the simplest possible ratios? It is evident that these notes will be expressed by the figures $1\frac{1}{2}$, $1\frac{1}{3}$, $1\frac{2}{3}$, $1\frac{1}{4}$, $1\frac{3}{4}$, &c., or by the ratios $\frac{3}{2}$, $\frac{4}{3}$, $\frac{5}{3}$, $\frac{5}{4}$, $\frac{7}{4}$, &c.

The simplest note is that of $\frac{3}{2}$, which corresponds to the ratio 2 : 3. It signifies that the new note makes three vibrations in the same time in which the fundamental note makes two, and represents also the harmony of the second and third harmonic. This ratio was recognised as consonant even by the ancient Greeks, who made it with scientific exaggeration the starting-point of their music and of the formation of the musical scale.

It is the harmony of the *fifth*. If the harmony 2 : 3 be taken, its resultant note is 1—that is to say, the octave below the fundamental note, seeing that this is equal to two. This resultant note contributes considerably to the improvement of the harmony of the fifth.

Another simple ratio is $\frac{4}{3}$, which may also be written 3 : 4. This ratio was also known to and admitted by the ancient Greeks. It is to a certain extent a consequence of the fifth, and can be derived from it; for if the fundamental note be 1, the fifth below it is evidently $\frac{2}{3}$, and its octave is obtained by doubling its value, hence we have $\frac{4}{3}$. This ratio is called in music the *fourth*, whence the fourth is the octave of the fifth below the fundamental note. In the harmonic series it represents the harmony of the third and fourth harmonic. Writing down the ratio 3 : 4, it is seen that the resultant note is 1, which does not correspond to any lower octave of the fundamental note, but is instead the second octave below the note 4—that is to say, of the fourth itself. The harmony of the fundamental note with the fourth presents, then, this somewhat strange character, that the resultant note, which arises from it, does not reinforce the fundamental note, but the fourth, and makes it to a certain extent more important than the fundamental note.

Another fairly simple ratio is that expressed by $\frac{5}{3}$; it corresponds to the *major sixth* in music. This ratio was unknown to the Greeks; it is, in fact, more complicated than the preceding, and it was some time before it was adopted. Indeed it presents this hitherto new character, that the resultant note reinforces neither the one or the other of the two notes, but is an altogether new note. Writing the ratio 3 : 5, the resultant note is 2, which is the fifth below the fundamental note 3.

Another important ratio is that furnished by the fourth and fifth harmonics, and expressed by $\frac{5}{4}$ or 4 : 5; it is called the major third. Written in the second manner, it gives as a resultant note 1—that is to say, the second octave below the fundamental note 4. It is a very important ratio, which was unknown to the ancient Greeks, and was introduced into modern music in the fifteenth and sixteenth centuries. The Greeks had in its stead the not widely different, but obviously dissonant harmony, $\frac{81}{64}$, formed from the fundamental note 1 by four successive fifths.

$$1,\ \tfrac{3}{2},\ \tfrac{3}{2}\times\tfrac{3}{2}=\tfrac{9}{4},\ \tfrac{3}{2}\times\tfrac{3}{2}\times\tfrac{3}{2}=\tfrac{27}{8}$$
$$\tfrac{3}{2}\times\tfrac{3}{2}\times\tfrac{3}{2}\times\tfrac{3}{2}=\tfrac{81}{16}$$

This note, lowered by two octaves in order to bring it near to the note 1, and to keep it in the same octave, becomes $\frac{81}{64}$, which is precisely the Greek third, also called the *Pythagorean* third, from the name of its inventor.

It may be said without exaggeration that the substitution for it of the consonant and harmonic third $\frac{5}{4}$, constitutes the most remarkable and most decisive progress of our scale as compared with that of the Greeks. The third $\frac{5}{4}$ also comes into the category of consonant harmonies through the consideration that its resultant note being the second octave below, reinforces the fundamental note. Another harmony, which was introduced into music, is the *minor third.* It is expressed by the ratio , or also 5 : 6. It was only adopted in the seventeenth century with many reservations, together with the harmony of the sixth, from which it can be easily derived. In fact, it is only the octave of the sixth inverted. As late as the middle of the last century, even in the compositions of Mozart, this harmony was considered as imperfect, and was avoided as far as possible as the final chord of a piece. The resultant note is very low, and does not reinforce either of the notes of the harmony. Writing it 5 : 6, the resultant note is 1, and is in respect to the note 6 of the harmony the second octave below its fifth. This note is very low, and not dissonant with the notes 5 and 6. But in the further combinations to which the harmony of the minor third becomes subjected, the resultant note, as will be seen later on, becomes obviously dissonant.

There is one other harmony, which is now considered consonant, although imperfectly so—that of the minor sixth $\frac{8}{5}$, or also 5 : 8. It was the last with that of the minor third to be adopted. The resultant note is 3—that is to say, the major sixth below the fundamental note 5—a new note which is not dissonant in itself, but which becomes so in the fuller chords to which the minor sixth gives rise.

10. This harmony of the minor sixth is evidently on the limit of dissonant notes. It may, however, be asked, if it would not be possible to push on farther in this direction, so as to enrich music with other fairly consonant harmonies. This is a question of high musical art, one which has latterly been much discussed, and one which would merit even deeper study. It is, however, perhaps too delicate a question to be touched on here. To treat it properly it would be necessary to enter into a series of most minute details, and to consider the harmonies in their relations to three

or four different notes. Such an investigation would go far beyond the limits of this treatise. It may, however, be observed that, in order to enlarge the field of music in this direction, it would be proper to have recourse to the seventh harmonic, and to consider the ratios $\frac{7}{4}$, $\frac{7}{5}$, $\frac{7}{6}$, $\frac{8}{7}$, &c., in which the seventh harmonic has a decisive importance. Some of these ratios—as $\frac{7}{4}$, $\frac{7}{6}$, $\frac{8}{7}$—are undoubtedly dissonant to our ears. Their resultant notes are so also, or are at great intervals, and therefore insignificant, and I do not believe that future generations will ever be taught to think otherwise. The same cannot be said *a priori* of the harmony $\frac{7}{5}$. But it is a strange phenomenon to observe how the seventh harmonic can be entirely banished from music even as a dissonant note, notwithstanding that much more complicated, and therefore much more dissonant, ratios are adopted, as, for example, $\frac{9}{8}$, $\frac{10}{9}$, &c., of which we shall speak hereafter. To an ear accustomed to our music, as it is, the seventh harmonic may appear like an unpleasant note; but an unprejudiced examination, according to the opinion of some—an opinion with which I entirely agree—shows that it is rather strange than unpleasant; that in certain special cases it affords very good discords and passing chords, and that the strangeness arises rather from our want of familiarity with it than from its inherent nature.

It need not, however, be a matter of surprise that this note should be thus banished from practical music. The reason is, scientifically speaking, that the number 7 is not sufficiently small for a consonant harmony, and that being great, it has the fault of being a prime number. Since, even in discords, it is of the greatest importance not to make too much use of such numbers, numbers greater than 7, but divisible by 2, 3, 4, or 5, have a great numerical advantage over it.* And this is the true and principal reason why no use is made of it in music.

Without wishing to push too far forward, and to prophesy what will happen in the future, it may be observed that the systematic introduction of the seventh harmonic into music would produce in it a very deep and almost incalculable revolution—a revolution which does not seem justifiable, because for our magnificent musical system another would be substituted, perhaps as magnificent, but certainly not better, and probably worse, and at any rate more artificial. This does not, however, exclude the possibility that a secondary part in the musical system will hereafter be assigned to the seventh harmonic. To certain chords—for example, the chord of the diminished seventh—and discords it is well suited, and may sometimes be substituted with advantage for some in present use.

However this may be, it is certain that for us the seventh harmonic represents the great line of demarcation between consonant harmonies and discords. Below it is

* *Euler* had remarked the importance of the numbers 2, 3, and 5, and established upon them a rule for the development of our musical system.

consonance, and above it dissonance, and between these is a great hiatus. We have thus the following harmonies in the interval of one octave:—

Perfectly consonant . . .	$\frac{3}{2}$	$\frac{4}{3}$
Consonant	$\frac{5}{3}$	$\frac{5}{4}$
Imperfectly consonant . .	$\frac{6}{5}$	$\frac{8}{5}$
Hiatus formed by the seventh harmonic.		
Dissonant	$\frac{9}{8}$	$\frac{10}{9}$, &c.

This demonstration may be terminated by representing in musical notation the harmonies examined above, with the resultant notes of the first order which arise from them. The harmonies will be found on the upper line, in the treble clef; the resultant notes on the lower line, in the bass clef.

This mode of illustration will serve to make what has been explained above more clear.

CHAPTER VI.

1. Helmholtz's double siren—2. Application of the law of simple ratio to three or more notes—3. Perfect major and minor chords, their nature—4. Their inversion.

1. The laws explained in the preceding chapter can be demonstrated by means of the siren constructed by Helmholtz, which is called the *double siren* (fig. 28). It is composed of two complete sirens, a_0, a_1, placed one over the other, so that their revolving discs face each other. These are attached to the same arbor k, and therefore turn together with the same velocity. In the middle of this arbor is the counter (not represented in the figure), which is intended to measure the number of turns when absolute measurement is required. Each disc carries four concentric circles of holes, according to an idea already realised by *Dove;* and by means of four buttons i any one of the circles of holes, or all simultaneously, can be set in action. There are thus eight notes, which can be produced at will, at the disposition of the experimenter.

A strong current of air, which can be caused to enter either siren at g_0 or g_1, produces, as in the simple siren, the rotation of the discs and the formation of the notes.

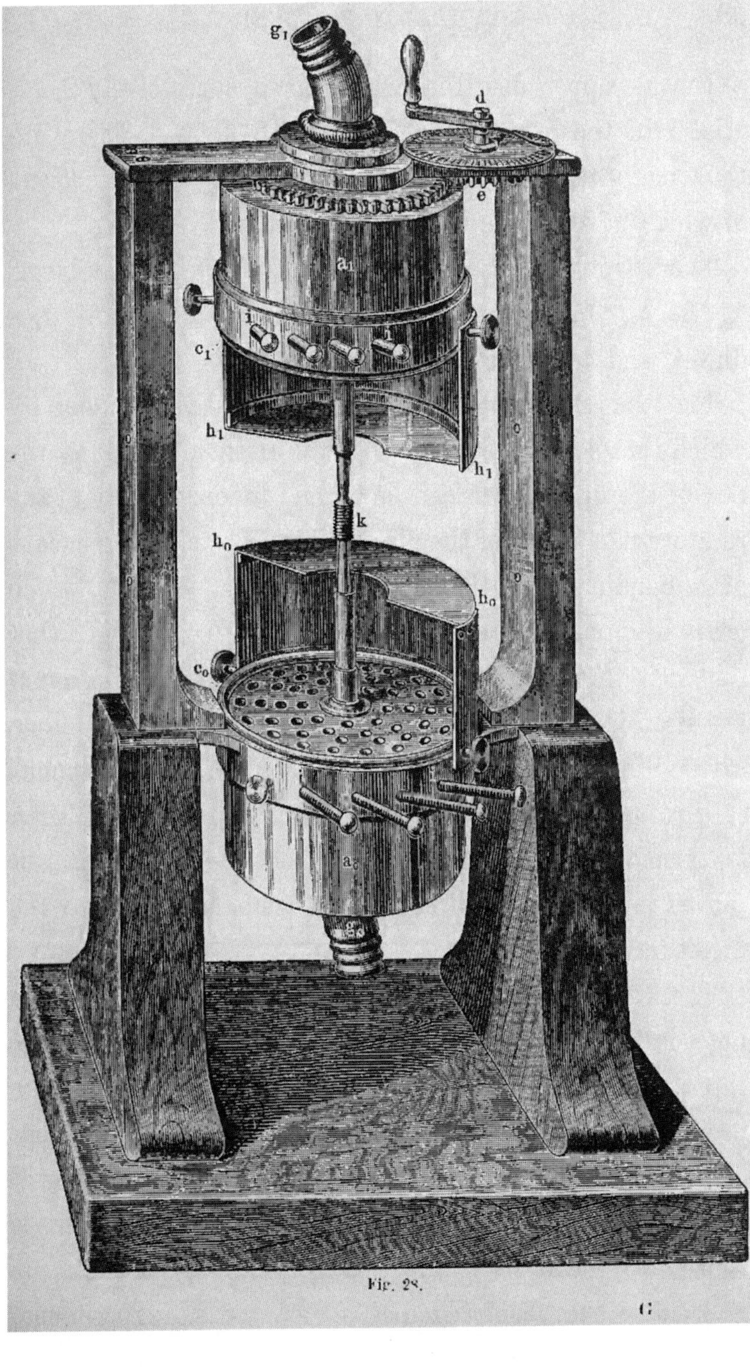

Fig. 28.

G

In the upper disc the circles have successively 9, 12, 15, 16, in the lower disc, 8, 10, 12, 18 holes. There are thus many possible combinations of notes, the vibrations of which have simple ratios to each other.

The revolving discs are covered by cylindrical boxes h_0, h_0, h_1, h_1, which serve to reinforce the notes produced, and to make them clearer.

For the study of beats there is an arrangement by which these ratios can be slightly altered. In fact, the box of the upper siren can be turned independently of the rotatory movement of the discs. This is attained by means of a handle *d*, which turns the toothed wheel *e*, which gears into one on the upper siren, and is so arranged that for each three turns there is one complete revolution of the siren itself. Under the handle is a graduated circle divided into sixteenths, whence each division corresponds to $\frac{1}{48}$ of a complete turn of the siren. So when the siren is turned, it follows the holes in the revolving disc, or moves in a contrary direction to them, according to the direction of the rotation.

The effect in the first case is to somewhat lower the note, in the second to raise it. The reason of this is, that the note depends on the number of puffs of air which are produced each time that the holes of the revolving disc coincide with the holes of the siren; these puffs will be more or fewer in number, according as the siren is caused to move in a direction contrary to, or the same as that of the revolving disc. Very varied experiments may be made by means of this double siren. The most important and the most interesting of them may now be described. If the twelve holes of both upper and lower siren be set in action, two identical notes are obtained. Their effects are added together, and they therefore give a reinforced note, when the two sirens are so placed that the puffs of air from both are made at the same instant.

But, on the other hand, they enfeeble each other when the two sirens are so placed that their puffs are alternate. If the handle *d* be slowly and regularly turned, the notes sometimes strengthen, sometimes weaken each other; beats are thus obtained, the number of which per second corresponds to the difference of the number of vibrations per second of the two notes produced by the sirens.

If the twelve holes of the two discs be kept in action, and the blower be more loaded, the siren will turn quicker, and the two notes will rise in pitch but will still remain in unison, which demonstrates that unison is independent of the absolute number of vibrations per second.

But if the eight and sixteen holes be set in action, a note and its octave is obtained, since the vibrations in any given time are as 1 to 2. The octave is quite perfect, and remains so, however much the velocity of rotation of the discs may be altered by loading the blower. The notes change, but their ratio remains the same. Whatever, then, may be the fundamental note, the octave always makes double the number of vibrations in a second. If it be desired to produce beats, the upper siren has but to be turned. The phenomenon which results is easy to foresee and to explain.

The ratio of the fifth can be produced in different ways by combining the numbers 8 and 12, 10 and 15, or 12 and 18, since in each case there is the ratio 2 : 3. The ratio of the fourth is obtained by the holes 9 and 12, 12 and 16; that of the major third by 8 and 10, 12 and 15, since they have the ratio 4 : 5.

The major and minor sixth are obtained by the combinations 9 and 15, and 10 and 16.

Lastly, the ratio of the minor third is obtained by the holes 10 and 12, 15 and 18.

There are many other combinations possible, but these examples are enough for the present purpose. The harmonies obtained by this means are mathematically correct, and therefore preferable to those obtained by other instruments. Experiments made with this instrument show clearly that the absolute number of vibrations per second has no influence on the harmonies, because the ratios always remain the same; since in this instrument the ratios are fixed by the number of holes in action, whilst the absolute number of vibrations per second depends on the velocity of rotation of the revolving discs, which can be controlled at will. The fundamental note, then, may be any note whatever; but when once a note has been decided on for this office, the number of vibrations per second of all the others is fixed by the ratios pointed out above.

Resultant notes also can be studied by means of this instrument. The laws are thus arrived at, which were set forth in the last chapter, by which the resultant note of a combination of any two notes was defined as a true difference note.

2. We must now treat of another question which is intimately connected with that just studied. As yet only the case of the combination of two notes has been considered, and the conditions under which they give a consonant chord. But the question may be generalised. It may be asked, Can three, four, or more notes be so combined as to produce a consonant chord? In this case the following rule holds good, which is nothing more than the generalisation of that explained and illustrated in the last chapter: *In order that a chord, produced by three or more notes, may be consonant, it is necessary that the different notes that compose it bear, in respect of the number per second of their vibrations, simple ratios not only to the fundamental note but also to each other.* This rule shows that in order to produce a consonant chord, it is not enough to take the most simple ratios of octave, fifth, fourth, &c., but it is necessary also to bear in mind that the different notes that compose it must bear simple ratios to each other. Thus, for example, a chord formed by the fundamental note, its fourth, fifth, and octave, is clearly dissonant, notwith-

standing that these notes are represented by the most simple ratios existing—

$$1, \tfrac{4}{3}, \tfrac{3}{2}, 2.$$

The reason is that the ratio of the fourth to the fifth is too complex, and therefore dissonant. In fact, this ratio is expressed by $\frac{9}{8}$, which ratio is not comprised amongst those giving consonant harmonies.

3. In this respect a much better chord is obtained by substituting the major third for the fourth, notwithstanding the fact that it has a more complex ratio with the fundamental note. We thus obtain the notes—

$$1, \tfrac{5}{4}, \tfrac{3}{2}, 2,$$

whose ratios are—

$$\tfrac{5}{4}, \tfrac{6}{5}, \tfrac{4}{3},$$

which are all consonant.

The above chord is the most consonant that exists in music, and it is therefore called the *perfect chord;* to which is also added the word *major*, because the major third forms part of it, and to distinguish it from the *perfect minor chord*, in which the minor third is substituted for the major third.

The perfect major chord, as its name expresses, is the most consonant chord that can be imagined. In its most simple form it is composed of the fundamental note, major third and fifth, and it is usual to add the octave. The ratios of these notes to each other are a major third, a minor third, and a fourth. The resultant notes which they form can be easily determined. In fact, writing the chord in figures—

$$1, \tfrac{5}{4}, \tfrac{3}{2}, 2,$$

by combining each note with all the others, it is seen that the resultant notes are the following:—

$$\tfrac{1}{4}, \tfrac{1}{2}, \tfrac{3}{4}, 1.$$

The first represents the second octave below the fundamental note; the second, the first octave below the same note; the third, the octave below the fifth; and the last, the fundamental note itself. Therefore the resultant notes reinforce existing notes, more especially the fundamental note, which contributes greatly to giving the chord a firm, bold, and decided character. In this respect the perfect minor chord is inferior to the first, although its structure is not very different. In fact, if it be written in the following manner:—

$$1, \tfrac{6}{5}, \tfrac{3}{2}, 2,$$

it will be seen that the ratios of the successive notes to each other are—

$$\tfrac{6}{5}, \tfrac{5}{4}, \tfrac{4}{3},$$

which only differ from those of the major chord by the order in which they follow each other. The ratios of the notes in the perfect major chord to each other are the intervals of a major third, a minor third and a fourth· whilst in the minor chord they are a minor third, a major third and a fourth. The difference is very small in itself, and is not enough to explain the great fundamental difference that exists between these two chords.

But a far more conclusive explanation is found by means of the resultant notes. These are in the perfect minor chord—

$$\tfrac{1}{5},\ \tfrac{3}{10},\ \tfrac{1}{2},\ \tfrac{4}{5},\ 1.$$

The first represents the major third below the second octave below the fundamental note, and is a new note in the chord, which is dissonant with the fifth; the second is the second octave below the minor third; the third is the octave below the fundamental note; the fourth is the major third below the fundamental note—that is to say, the second octave above the first resultant note—which thus adds to the existing dissonance of the chord; the last finally reinforces the fundamental note.

Whilst, then, all the resultant notes in the perfect major chord reinforce the existing harmony, certain of them in the minor chord tend to disturb it. If these resultant notes were stronger, they would suffice to make the chord dissonant. Even as it is, they impart to it a disturbed and undecided character.

These two perfect chords, the major and the minor, form the keystone of our musical system. They are often met with in compositions, and every piece of music must end with one or the other.

They are, in truth, the fundamental chords, and impart to the composition its special character. Pieces founded on the perfect major chord have a cheerful, brisk, bold, open character, and are therefore well adapted for the expression of such conditions of the mind. On the other hand, those founded on the perfect minor chord are sad and melancholy, or to express it more exactly, are disturbed and undecided, and therefore express well conditions of the mind in which uncertainty and indecision play the greatest part. Thus it is seen that theory and practice perfectly agree in defining these two fundamental chords. It may be added that the history of music also corroborates these views. Whilst the perfect major chord has been accepted from the very birth of harmonised music properly so called, the perfect minor chord was considered for a long time rather as a slightly dissonant passing chord than as a fundamental chord. Up to the time of Sebastian Bach—that is, up to the middle of the last century—there were those who would hesitate to conclude a piece of music with the minor chord, even when its character demanded it. In Mozart we find a certain reluctance to use it as a closing chord; his predecessors willingly omitted the minor third, which probably did not sound well enough to them. It may almost be said that the most highly gifted musical natures may have, as it were, felt beforehand that which theory has since been able to explain in a simple and conclusive way. To make this more clear with respect to the resultant notes of the two perfect chords, these notes are given below, written in the musical notation. On the first line are the two chords, on the second the resultant notes of the first order which they generate. Those of the first order only are considered, because those of higher orders are only heard under exceptional circumstances, and have no great practical importance.

PERFECT CHORD.

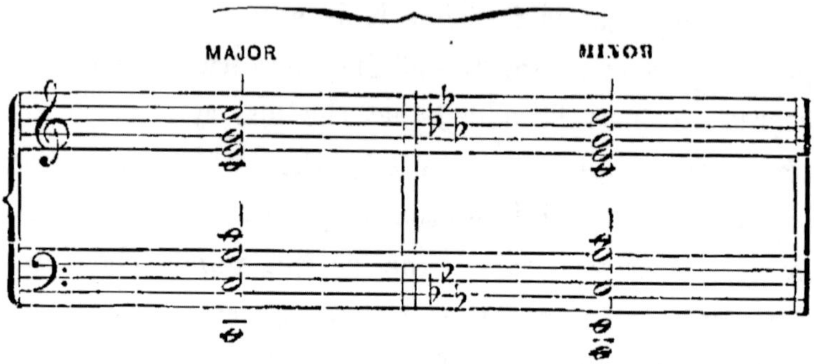

4. The perfect chord can, however, be used in different ways. Carrying one or more of the notes an octave higher or lower is called inverting the chord. The chord then acquires a somewhat different character from that which it had at first, and the resultant notes especially are considerably modified. This is a point which can be only indicated, as a fuller study of it would require wider limits than those of this treatise. However, it may be remarked that music is very rich in this respect, and that inverted chords constituted the principal resource of *Palestrina,* and of the composers of his school and time. Chords which in a given position have consonant resultant notes, can be transformed by invertion into others with more or less dissonant resultant notes. This is especially the case with the perfect minor chord, in which the slight existing dissonance can be considerably reinforced

by means of invertion, and can be transformed into a much more marked dissonance. *Palestrina,* who had certainly one of the most finely gifted musical organisations, made very great use of this musical process; and it is wonderful to see how, without being guided by theory, and only by the delicacy of his ear, he has been able to feel and to appreciate such slight differences. In his music he makes but very little use of true dissonances, but, on the other hand, much use of those secondary dissonances which are produced by the resultant notes by means of invertions of the chords. This justifies the saying of a great German thinker, who called *Palestrina's* music, "music of angels, grieving indeed over things terrestrial, but not disturbing themselves on that account in their celestial serenity." As an example, a few inverted chords

are given with their resultant notes, taking the simplest case of three notes. The other cases are too complicated to find room here.

Besides the perfect chords, major and minor, there are also other simple chords. Amongst these may be mentioned the chord formed by the fundamental note, fourth, sixth, and octave, and that of the fundamental note with the third, sixth, and octave, which have characters differing somewhat from each other, and especially when they are compared with the perfect major or minor chord. These chords can be studied by the same rules as the perfect chords, and the conclusion is easily arrived at, that they are nothing more than these last suitably inverted, as is also seen by the example in musical notation on the preceding page.

CHAPTER VII.

1. DISCORDS—2 AND 3. THE NATURE OF MUSIC AND MUSICAL SCALES—4. ANCIENT MUSIC—5. GREEK SCALE—6. SCALE OF PYTHAGORAS—7. ITS DECAY—8. AMBROSIAN AND GREGORIAN CHANTS—9. POLYPHONIC MUSIC, HARMONY, THE PROTESTANT REFORMATION, PALESTRINA—10. CHANGE OF THE MUSICAL SCALE, THE TONIC, AND FUNDAMENTAL CHORD—11. THE MAJOR SCALE, MUSICAL INTERVALS—12. THE MINOR SCALE—13. KEY AND TRANSPOSITION—14 AND 15. SHARPS AND FLATS—16. THE TEMPERATE SCALE, ITS INACCURACY—17. DESIRABILITY OF ABANDONING IT.

1. UP to this point only the case of consonant chords has been considered; but music would be very poor if it were limited to these, and to the few notes that compose them. It may further be said that music formed only of consonant chords would be extremely monotonous and quite without vigour; it would be a sort of lullaby only intended to catch the ear without touching the mind, and without expressing anything.

To increase their resources, and to acquire greater vigour and strength in the expression of their ideas, musicians have been obliged to have recourse to dissonant notes and chords.

Strictly speaking, much greater satisfaction is felt when a dissonant chord is resolved into a consonant chord than when nothing but consonant chords has been heard. It is the force of contrast which produces these sensations in us, just as we doubly appreciate a calm after a storm.

This is exactly the idea which has unconsciously guided music up to our time. Its strength lies in dissonances, if they do not last too long, and they be at last resolved into consonant chords.

The perfect chord being the most consonant of all, must necessarily close the piece of music. There can be no absolute rule for the admission of dissonance, and for determining the limit up to which it may be used. All this depends on the degree of musical culture and on habit. Discords which now are perfectly permissible would have appeared monstrosities in the time of Palestrina. On the other hand, certain notes adopted by the Greeks at a period of decline—as, for example, quarter tones—are decisively rejected by us. It is therefore an error which many commit, to think that music, and especially modern music, has absolute character and values, and therefore to reject every musical system which does not agree with ours. There is nothing absolute in it but the laws of notes and their combinations; but the application of these laws is rather vague, and there remains a very wide and indeterminate field, which will be traversed in very different ways by different nations at various historical epochs.

2. If the history of music be examined with attention, even if all the evidence possible concerning the music of barbarous nations be collected, this constant phenomenon

will be found, that music proceeds by notes clearly separated from one another. Among the immense number of notes adopted for musical purposes, there are only a few that go to make up the various musical systems. A style of music in which it would be necessary to pass from one note to another, through all the intermediate notes, would become almost intolerable. It is true that our singers, and violin and violoncello players, sometimes make use of this style with success. But the slide from one note to another is only tolerated when it is used sparingly; and it always remains doubtful whether it would not be better to forbear from it entirely. Music proceeds, then, by musical *intervals*, precisely as a man walks with separate, firm, and decided steps. It seems that it is in its movement by intervals and by rhythmic steps, as also by the different shades of *piano* and *forte*, *crescendo* and *diminuendo*, *accelerando* and *rallantando*, of *legato* and *staccato*, which constitute musical accent, that the secret of the great impression which music makes upon the human heart resides. It has thus very varied means of completely adapting itself to the psychological movements which constitute any given state of mind, because it is to be observed that music does not express determinate sentiments; however, it is applicable to certain states of mind from which a special sentiment may arise. That this is the case is easily seen from instrumental music; the determinate sentiment is added by means of words united with music. But if the words be taken away, or modified in meaning, it will be seen that the same melody and the same music may be adapted to widely different sentiments.

Music is certainly the least material of all the fine arts. There is no question in it, as in sculpture, of copying idealised nature; nor, as in painting, of uniting to the study of nature the geometrical idea of perspective, and the optical idea of colours and their contrasts. Even architecture has a larger basis in nature itself. The trunks of trees and their branches, the grotto, the cavern, have suggested to the architect the first principles of his art, dictated to him by the wants of man and the conditions of the strength of materials; but in music nature offers scarcely anything. It is true that it abounds in musical sounds, but the idea of musical interval is but little suggested by the song of birds, and the idea of simple ratios is almost entirely wanting, and without these two ideas no music can exist. Man has therefore been obliged to create for himself his own instrument, and this is the reason why music has attained its full development so much later than its sister arts. Music resembles architecture more than any other art, as in it also numerical relations are considered. In fact, the height and width of a building or of a room, the height and width of windows, the thickness and height of columns—in a word, all dimensions are linked together by numerical relation. But these are only approximate relations which allow of a certain amount of freedom, whilst in music the relations must be exact, and nature revenges itself by beats whenever this fundamental law is departed from, however slightly.

3. In the music of all nations two unfailing characters are found, rhythmic movement and procedure by determinate intervals. The first appertains also to the speech and other acts of man, as walking, swimming, dancing, &c.; the second belongs exclusively to music.

All nations have selected notes to be used, have collected together those intended to be together, and have thus created one or more *musical scales.*

By musical scale is meant the collection of all the notes, comprised between the fundamental note and its octave, which succeed each other, and are intended to succeed each other, with a certain pre-established regularity. The study of the musical scale gives one of the most important and concise means of judging of the musical state of a nation. The examination of the musical scale is then of the greatest assistance, and for this reason a few hints will here be given on the most important musical systems that history has noticed up to the present time.

It seems strange that a few notes put together in a musical scale should be able to acquire a true importance in the study of music. If it were a question of an assemblage of notes made at hazard or capriciously, the matter would be of no importance; but the musical scale is always the product of the musical activity of many centuries. It is not established before music, but is developed with it. A very perfect form of music must have a very perfect scale; an imperfect and primitive form of music, on the other hand, will have a scale of little value.

In this respect, also, the comparison with architecture holds good.* In Greek architecture, the distances between column and column, and wall and wall, were small; the roofs were flat. Everything therefore was reducible to vertical and horizontal lines, and it is this great simplicity that constitutes one of the most beautiful characteristics of this form of architecture. The ancient Etruscans invented the arch, which allows of greater dimensions without impairing stability, and from which comes the vaulted roof, and as a more magnificent form of this, the dome.

The Roman architecture is founded on this new discovery. But the semicircular arch becomes unstable when of large dimensions; it is found that the pointed arch answers the purpose better in certain cases. It allows of and demands greater height in the buildings, and is accompanied by an admirable development of details which are perfectly adapted to it, and it is thus that the Gothic style in all its immense variety was developed. Thus a simple consideration of stability and strength has caused different nations to find different solutions, and from three simple primitive forms, three magnificent styles of architecture have been developed, which differ from

* Helmholtz, *Op. cit.*

each other so much that it would almost be thought that they had nothing in common.

4. Primitive music is as ancient as history itself. From the high plains of Asia, where many ancient historical traces of it are found, it followed man in his wanderings through China, India, and Egypt. One of the most ancient books, the Bible, speaks of music often and from its earliest pages.*

David and Solomon were very musical. They composed psalms full of inspiration, and evidently intended to be sung. To the latter is due the magnificent organisation of the singing in the temple at Jerusalem. He founded a school for singers, and a considerable band, which at last reached the number of four thousand trumpeters, the principal instruments being the harp, the cithern, the trumpet, and the drum.

The history of the development of Greek music has a more important bearing on the question now under consideration. It is incontestably established that the Greeks had no true principle of harmony even in their most prosperous times. The only thing that they did in this respect was to accompany in octaves when men and boys executed the same melody.

Thus their instrumentation only served to reinforce the

* [At Genesis iv. 21, speaking of the generations of Cain, it says: "And his brother's name was Jubal. He was the father of all such as handle the harp and organ." These words do not prove in the least that the organ was in existence at that time, but they are certainly characteristic.]

voice part, whether it were played in unison or in octaves, or whether more or less complicated variations were executed between one verse and another, or even between the parts of a verse. With them music was an auxiliary art, intended to increase, by idealising it, the effect of words.

The development of their music must be regarded only from this point of view, and in this respect it must be admitted that they arrived at a considerable degree of perfection, notwithstanding the truly primitive form under which it appears at the present time. It was, in fact, a sort of lofty declamation, with more variable rhythm and more frequent and more pronounced modulation than ordinary declamation. This music was much enjoyed by the Greeks, and when it is considered that the Greeks were the most artistic and most creative nation that has ever existed, it becomes necessary to look with care for the refinements which their music must, and in fact does contain.

5. The Greek musical scale was developed by successive fifths. Raising a note to its fifth signifies, as has been seen in the fifth chapter, multiplying its number of vibrations per second by $\frac{3}{2}$. This principle was rigorously maintained by the Greeks; rigorously, because the fourth, of which they made use from the very beginning, is only the fifth below the fundamental note raised an octave. To make the tracing out of these musical ideas clearer, recourse will be had to our modern nomenclature, making the supposition that our scale, which will be

studied later on in its details, is already known to the reader; calling the fundamental note *c*, and the successive notes of our scale *d*, *e*, *f*, *g*, *a*, *b*, *c*, with the terms sharps and flats for the intermediate notes, as is done in our modern music. In this scale the first note, the *c*, represents the fundamental note, the others are successively the second, the third, the fourth, the fifth, the sixth, the seventh, and the octave, according to the position which they occupy in the musical scale.

If the *c* be taken as a point of departure, its fifth is *g*, and its fifth below is *f*. If this last note be raised an octave, so as to bring it nearer to the other notes, and if the octave of *c* be also added, the following four notes are obtained:—

$$c, f, g, c,$$

whose musical ratios are—

$$1, \tfrac{4}{3}, \tfrac{3}{2}, 2.$$

These four notes, according to an ancient tradition, constituted the celebrated *lyre of Orpheus*. Musically speaking, it is certainly very poor, but the observation is interesting, that it contains the most important musical intervals of declamation. In fact, when an interrogation is made, the voice rises a fourth. To emphasise a word, it rises another tone, and goes to the fifth. In ending a story, it falls a fifth, &c. Thus it may be understood that Orpheus' lyre, notwithstanding its poverty, was well suited to a sort of musical declamation.

Progress by fifths up and down can be further continued.

The fifth of *g* is *d*, and if it be lowered an octave, its musical ratio will be $\frac{9}{8}$. The fifth below *f* is *b*♭, whence its musical ratio when raised an octave is $\frac{16}{9}$. We have then the following scale:—

c, d, f, g, b♭*, c,*

whose intervals are—

$$1, \frac{9}{8}, \frac{4}{3}, \frac{3}{2}, \frac{16}{9}, 2,$$

which is nothing more than a succession of fifths, all transposed into the same octave, in the following way:—

b♭, *f, c, g, d.*

This is the ancient Scotch and Chinese scale, in which an enormous number of popular songs are written, especially those of Scotland and Ireland, which all have a peculiar and special colouring.

6. But the scale can be continued further by successive fifths. Omitting, as the Greeks did, the fifth below *b*♭, and adding instead three successive fifths upwards, we shall have *a* as the fifth of *d*, and *e* as the fifth of *a*; and finally, *b* as the fifth of *e*.

The ratios of these notes, when brought into the same octave, will be—

$$\frac{27}{16}, \frac{81}{64}, \frac{243}{128},$$

whence the scale will be the following:—

c, d, e, f, g, a, b, c,

with the ratios—

$$1, \frac{9}{8}, \frac{81}{64}, \frac{4}{3}, \frac{3}{2}, \frac{27}{16}, \frac{243}{128}, 2.$$

The first and the second of the last three fifths mentioned above, the *a* and the *e*, were introduced by *Ter-*

pandro; the last, the *b*, by Pythagoras, whence the Greek scale still bears the name of the Pythagorean scale. It is formed, as has been seen, by successive fifths—that is to say, with the fundamental idea of simple ratios.

But it is necessary to observe that the execution of this idea is not entirely happy. It is true that the law of formation is very simple, but the individual notes have, nevertheless, an origin very distant from the fundamental note. The mode of formation of the scale was well suited for tuning the strings of the lyre, and this seems to have been one of the principal motives for adopting this mode of formation; but the interval between any two notes of the scale is anything but simple. It may thus be seen further that some of the notes bear extremely complex ratios to the fundamental note.

This is especially the case with the three notes last introduced into the scale—that is to say, those corresponding to our *a*, *e*, and *b*—which no longer bear simple ratios to the fundamental note, being expressed by the fractions $\frac{27}{16}$, $\frac{81}{64}$, $\frac{243}{128}$.

The last would not be a matter of much importance. The *b* can only be considered as a passing note, which by its open dissonance leads up to the *c*, or other consonant note. Its being more or less dissonant does no harm, and may in certain cases be pleasing. But that the third and sixth bear complex ratios is a grave defect, and this is probably the principal reason why the Greek music did not develop harmony. The Pythagorean third and sixth are decidedly dissonant, and with the fourth and fifth alone no development of harmony is possible, the more so that the interval between the fourth and fifth is rather small, and therefore dissonant.

7. The Pythagorean scale held almost exclusive sway in Greece. However, in the last centuries before the Christian era—that is to say, during the period of Greek decline in politics and art—many attempts at modifying it are found. Thus, for example, they divided the interval between the notes corresponding to our *c* and *d* into two parts, introducing a note in the middle. At last they went so far as to again divide these intervals in two, thus introducing the *quarter tone,* which we look upon as discordant. Others again introduced various intervals, founded for the most part rather on theoretical speculations than on artistic sentiment.

All these attempts have left no trace behind them, and therefore are of no importance. But the Pythagorean scale passed from Greece to Italy, where it held sovereign sway up to the sixteenth century, at which epoch began its slow and successive transformation into our two musical scales.

It ought to be added that the Greeks, in order to increase the musical resources of their scale, also formed from it several different scales, which are distinguished from the first only by the point of departure.

The law of formation was very simple; in fact, suppose the scale written as follows:—

c, d, e, f, g, a, b, c.

Any note whatever may be taken as a starting-point, and the scale may be written, for example, thus—

e, f, g, a, b, c, d, e;

or—

a, b, c, d, e, f, g, a, &c.

It is evident that seven scales in all can be formed in this way, which were not all used by the Greeks at different epochs, but which were all possible. A musical piece, founded on one or other of them, must evidently have had a distinctive character; and it is in this respect, in the blendings of shades, that Greek melody must be considered as more rich than ours, which is subject to far more rigid rules.

8. The different Greek scales underwent much disturbance in Italy. *Ambrose*, Bishop of Milan, and later, *Pope Gregory the Great*, had the merit of re-establishing the first four; and the second, the rest of the Greek scales. Thus ecclesiastical music [the Ambrosian and Gregorian chants] acquired a clearer and more elevated character. It was a recitative on a long-sustained or short note, according to the words that accompanied it, music for a single voice, which is still partially retained, and which may be said to differ from the Greek music only by the purpose for which it is intended.

9. In the tenth and eleventh centuries an attempt was begun, especially in Flanders, at *polyphonic* music—that is to say, at music for several voices. It consisted in

combining together two different melodies, so as not to produce discord. This sort of music also advanced rapidly in Italy. In the time of *Guido d'Arezzo*, the celebrated inventor of musical notation, such pieces were composed, in which frequent use was made of successive fifths—a thing most displeasing to the ear, and which we now look upon as a serious mistake in music. By the impulse of *Josquino* and *Orlando Tasso*, the last and perhaps the most important composer of that school, polyphonic music was developed in a surprising manner. Three, four, and more melodies were combined together in a most complicated fashion, in which the art of combination had a much more considerable part than artistic inspiration—mere *tours de force* without any musical worth! Such music was especially cultivated by church singers, to whom was thus given a means of displaying their own ability. The voices were interwoven in a thousand ways, and the only restraint on the composer was not to produce unpleasant discords. Luther's great Reformation put an end to this fictitious and artificial style of music. Protestantism rising into importance at that time, made it a necessity that church singing should be executed by the congregation, and not by a special class of singers. The music was therefore obliged to be simplified to put it within the power of all. The ground was already prepared for this. The Troubadours, Minstrels, and Minnesänger had developed primitive and simple melody, whence sprang madrigals and popular songs. And thus for polyphonic music another form was substituted, in which the different voices sustain each other.

Harmony properly so called arose from these simple and sustained chords, and from the easy movement of the different voice parts.

The shock of the German movement was felt even in Italy, where musical reform was initiated in a truly genial way by *Palestrina*, partly, indeed, to follow the deliberations of the Council of Trent. *Palestrina* abandoned the artificial method in use up to that time, and laid the most stress on simplicity and deeply-artistic inspiration. His compositions ("Crux fidelis," "Improperia," "Missa papæ Marcelli," &c.) are, and always will be, a model of that style.

10. But so radical a transformation could not be brought about by one individual, nor in a short time. The Pythagorean scale, which was in general use at the time, was opposed to a true development of harmony, and the more so when the execution of the music was intrusted to human voices in which every discord becomes doubly perceptible. True harmony could only be developed by means of the successive transformations of the musical scale into another, in which the ratios of the notes to the fundamental note, and to each other, were as simple as possible. It is thus that the different Greek scales have been transformed by degrees into our two modern scales—that is, into the *major scale* and the *minor scale*. The first was more easily to be found, but the second, with its two variations for the ascending and descending movement, is

not found completely developed until the seventeenth century, when music had attained an admirable degree of development, and when there were magnificent schools of music and singing in the principal cities of Italy.

Yet another idea characterises our modern music: the idea of the fundamental note and chord. This idea did not exist in Greek music, although certain passages of *Aristotle* point to something similar. It did not exist in the Ambrosian chant, but began to be developed with polyphonic music. The interlaced singing of the Middle Ages demanded, as a practical condition, that the different singers should frequently return to one note, as to a firm resting-place, in order to keep together. The more complicated the harmony was, the more necessary such a resting-place became. It is thus that the idea of the *fundamental note* or *tonic* was developed, and later, the idea of the fundamental chord and of key. This precept has become more and more rigid, as music has become more complicated. It is now required that a piece of music should begin and end with the fundamental chord, which can only be a perfect major or minor chord, and that in the following out of the musical idea, and in the development of the great masses of chorus and orchestra the fundamental note should often recur, as a necessary resting-place for our comprehension.

This idea was only slowly developed. In the music of *Palestrina* and of his successors it had not reached that clearness which is required at the present day. And this is perhaps the principal reason why this music, notwithstanding its simplicity and great beauty, appears somewhat confused, and rather quaint than beautiful.

11. These facts being premised, it is now time to examine in detail the formation and the properties of our musical scale, as they have been thus necessarily developed by the requirements of polyphonic music and of harmony. The scales which are adopted now are two in number: the *major scale* and the *minor scale.* The last having yet another modification, which may be considered as the point where the one passes into the other.

In order to hear our scale in its most perfect possible form, use may be made of an instrument (fig. 29) invented by *Seebeck* and perfected by *König.* A strong clockwork movement, enclosed in a box P, enables a regular movement of rotation to be given to a metallic disc placed at O. The disc carries eight series of holes, placed concentrically to the same circle at equal distances from each other. Tubes of indiarubber, A, B, C, are so arranged that any circle of holes can be blown against at will, so as to produce different notes. It is, in fact, a siren in which the rotatory movement is produced independently of the current of air. The eight circles, beginning with the inner one, have the following numbers of holes:—

24, 27, 30, 32, 36, 40, 45, 48.

But as the number of vibrations per second of the notes produced is proportional to the number of impulses, and this to the number of holes, it follows that at equal velocities the above numbers will express the relative number of the vibrations. Dividing by 24, the following ratios are obtained:—

$$1, \frac{9}{8}, \frac{5}{4}, \frac{4}{3}, \frac{3}{2}, \frac{5}{3}, \frac{15}{8}, 2.$$

When the disc has acquired a uniform velocity, if the

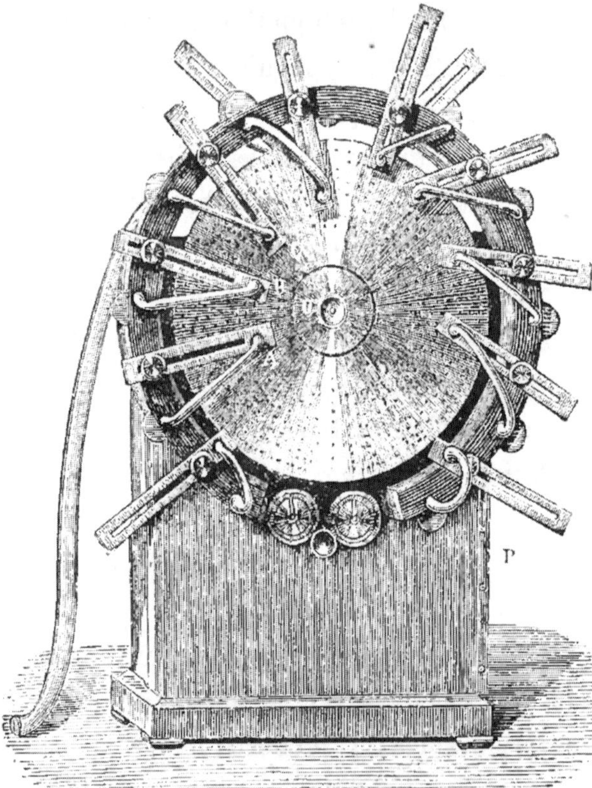

Fig. 29.

different circles of holes be successively blown against, it will be heard that the major scale is obtained. And it may be added that this scale is perfect, because it satisfies, even in theory, the law of exact ratios.

The major scale is therefore constituted by the following ratios:—

$$1, \frac{9}{8}, \frac{5}{4}, \frac{4}{3}, \frac{3}{2}, \frac{5}{3}, \frac{15}{8}, 2,$$

which are called—

c, d, e, f, g, a, b, c.

In it, as may be seen, the major third, $\frac{5}{4}$, the fourth, $\frac{4}{3}$, the fifth, $\frac{3}{2}$, the sixth, $\frac{5}{3}$, form consonant harmonies with the fundamental note, which harmonies have already been deduced from theory. They are the most simple ratios which can be mentioned. It may further be seen that these ratios have been substituted with advantage for some of the more complicated ones of the Pythagorean scale; especially the third and the sixth, which in it were dissonant, and which are now consonant. The second, $\frac{9}{8}$, is the same as in the Pythagorean scale; the seventh, $\frac{15}{8}$, is considerably simplified. It may be said, then, that this scale is nothing more than a modification of the Pythagorean scale, made with the idea of keeping the same notes in such a form, however, that they should satisfy the law of simple ratio. It is clear and evident that this scale must therefore lend itself to harmony, whilst the Pythagorean scale was decidedly opposed to it.

But it is not enough that the ratio of the note to the fundamental note should be simple, it is necessary that the ratios of the notes to each other should also be simple. It will not be possible in this treatise to examine the question with all the necessary details; the most remarkable properties of our major scale may, however, be made known. The ratio between one note of the scale and its antecedent note is called a musical *interval*, a ratio which is found by dividing one by the other. In this respect the comparison with the Pythagorean scale is very instructive. The Pythagorean scale is expressed by the following ratios:—

$$1, \tfrac{9}{8}, \tfrac{81}{64}, \tfrac{4}{3}, \tfrac{3}{2}, \tfrac{27}{16}, \tfrac{243}{128}, 2.$$

The intervals are therefore as follows:—

$$\tfrac{9}{8}, \tfrac{9}{8}, \tfrac{256}{243}, \tfrac{9}{8}, \tfrac{9}{8}, \tfrac{9}{8}, \tfrac{256}{243}.$$

On this scale, therefore, the intervals are of two classes: the one a somewhat large interval, $\frac{9}{8}$, which is called a *whole tone;* the other smaller and more complicated, $\frac{256}{243}$, which is called a *semitone.* The Pythagorean scale is composed of five whole tones all equal to each other, and of two complicated semitones, one placed between the third and fourth, the other between the seventh and octave.

Our major scale has the following ratios:—

$$1, \tfrac{9}{8}, \tfrac{5}{4}, \tfrac{4}{3}, \tfrac{3}{2}, \tfrac{5}{3}, \tfrac{15}{8}, 2.$$

Its intervals are—

$$\tfrac{9}{8}, \tfrac{10}{9}, \tfrac{16}{15}, \tfrac{9}{8}, \tfrac{10}{9}, \tfrac{9}{8}, \tfrac{16}{15}.$$

In it the intervals are therefore of three classes: the largest, $\frac{9}{8}$, which occur three times, are the same as the Pythagorean intervals; others, a little smaller, $\frac{10}{9}$, are met with twice. They are both called *whole tones,* but to distinguish one from the other, $\frac{9}{8}$ is called a *major tone,* and $\frac{10}{9}$ a *minor tone.* The third interval, considerably smaller than the two first, $\frac{16}{15}$, is met with twice, and in the same place as the Pythagorean interval $\frac{256}{243}$. It is called a major *semitone*, to distinguish it from another smaller semitone, $\frac{25}{24}$, which will be spoken of later on, and which is called a minor semitone. If no distinction be made between the major and minor tone, it will be seen that the major scale presents, like the Pythagorean, five tones, and two semitones, distributed in the same order. The difference between the two scales lies in this, that we make a distinction between the major and minor tone, and that our semitone is much more simple than the Pythagorean. We have thus three different intervals instead of two, and therefore a greater complication, which however is amply compensated for by the simpler ratios and intervals. To this may be added that the greater complication which has been pointed out constitutes even by itself a greater variety, and hence a greater richness, in our music.

Certain musical niceties—as, for example, the somewhat different character possessed by the different keys—find their most natural explanation in this greater variety of musical intervals; and in truth, since, for example, the interval between *c* and *d* is not equal to that between *d* and *e*, to play *c d* is not the same thing as to play *d e*. The same reasoning applied to a whole piece of music, shows that the selection of the first fundamental note and of the key modifies somewhat the order of the intervals, and thence also the musical character of the piece.

12. The second of our scales is the minor scale, in which the minor third is substituted for the major third, and the sixth and seventh are modified. It is composed of the following ratios:—

$$1,\ \tfrac{9}{8},\ \tfrac{6}{5},\ \tfrac{4}{3},\ \tfrac{3}{2},\ \tfrac{8}{5},\ \tfrac{9}{5},\ 2.$$

Its intervals are the following:—

$$\tfrac{9}{8},\ \tfrac{16}{15},\ \tfrac{10}{9},\ \tfrac{9}{8},\ \tfrac{16}{15},\ \tfrac{9}{8},\ \tfrac{10}{9}.$$

In it the same intervals are found as in the major scale; the interval $\frac{9}{8}$ three times, $\frac{10}{9}$ twice, and $\frac{16}{15}$ twice. The minor scale, then, only differs from the major in that the same intervals are differently distributed.

The minor scale is also used in the following form:—

$$1,\ \tfrac{9}{8},\ \tfrac{6}{5},\ \tfrac{4}{3},\ \tfrac{3}{2},\ \tfrac{5}{3},\ \tfrac{15}{8},\ 2.$$

In which the intervals are—

$$\tfrac{9}{8},\ \tfrac{16}{15},\ \tfrac{10}{9},\ \tfrac{9}{8},\ \tfrac{10}{9},\ \tfrac{9}{8},\ \tfrac{16}{15}.$$

This scale is composed, for the first half, of the minor scale, and for the second half, of the major scale. The intervals are again the same, only differently distributed. The second form is adopted by preference for the ascending scale—that is to say, for the movement from bass towards treble—whilst the first form is adopted for the descending scale, from treble to bass.

The minor scale, then, has as its characteristic note the minor third, whilst the major scale has the major third. These two scales may therefore be considered as the further development of, and emanation from, the perfect major and minor chords, with which they are closely allied. A piece of music, written in the major scale, has the major chord as its basis; the minor chord is reserved for those pieces which move within the minor scale.

The characteristic difference between the two scales lies in the thirds. Now the interval between the major third, $\frac{5}{4}$, and the minor third, $\frac{6}{5}$, is found by dividing one by the other. It is, then, $\frac{25}{24}$, a smaller interval than the major semitone, $\frac{16}{15}$; and on this account is called the *minor semitone.* It may therefore be concluded that the whole of the great difference which exists between the major and minor scale may be reduced to the presence or absence of *one minor semitone* in the interval of the third. However small this difference may be mathematically speaking, it is very great from an artistic point of view. Those points discussed with respect to the two perfect chords [see chapter vi.] also hold good for the two scales. The major scale and all pieces founded on it have an open, cheerful, bold character; pieces that are based on the minor scale are sad, melancholy, and, above all, undecided. The reason for this is to be found in the different resultant notes, which are produced by the two perfect chords; they are also again met with in the scales. In conclusion, it may be said that variations so small as to appear unimportant considerably modify the character of a piece of music.

In this respect the scale is like the skeleton of organised beings, who show different characters, tendencies, and developments as soon as characteristic differences are set up in its construction.

13. One last step remained to be made in music, and it is not probable that it is as yet entirely made. The scale must now be considered from a fresh point of view, when it will be seen that it is infinitely richer in resource than would be at first sight imagined.

This step consists of transposition, and of modulating from one key to another in the most artistic manner.

Consider an instrument with fixed notes, such as the pianoforte, and suppose that the scale begins on *c*, and that some piece of music—for example, a melody—is founded on this scale. Its fundamental note or tonic is then *c*. But it may happen that a singer who is to execute this melody finds it too low or too high for his voice, and he prefers to transpose it, so that the tonic may be, for example, *g*.

This is permissible, since it has been seen as a general proposition that any note, whatever may be its number of vibrations per second, may be used as a point of departure, since all the successive notes remain in determinate ratios to the first or fundamental note; which signifies, with respect to the scale, that the intervals remain the same when the tonic is moved from *c* to *g*.

Now, if the major scale be examined, it will be found that if the fundamental note be *c*, there is the interval of a semitone between *e* and *f*—that is to say, between the third and fourth; the same interval is found between *b* and *c*, or between the seventh and octave. If the piece, then, be transposed from *c* to *g*, in order not to alter the disposition of the semitones, it must be referred to a scale which begins on *g*, and has the interval of a semitone between the third and fourth, and seventh and octave. But if this scale be written simply in the following way, as the Greeks wrote theirs:—

g, *a*, *b*, *c*, *d*, *e*, *f*, *g*,

it will be seen that between the third and fourth—that is, between *b* and *c*—there is the required interval of a semitone. This is not, however, the case between the seventh and octave—that is, between *f* and *g*. The semitone is, on the other hand, found between the sixth and seventh—that is to say, between *e* and *f*. The scale, then, does not preserve the original order of the intervals. The desired order of intervals can, however, easily be obtained by raising *f* a semitone, since then the interval between the sixth and seventh becomes a tone, whilst that between the seventh and octave becomes a semitone.

14. Raising a note a semitone signifies raising that note to its *sharp*, as lowering it a semitone signifies lowering it to its *flat*. In theory, raising a note to its sharp means multiplying the number of vibrations per second of that note by the ratio $\frac{25}{24}$, which is the ratio of the number of vibrations per second of two notes at an interval of a minor semitone. To lower it to its flat, on the other hand, means to multiply its number of vibrations per second by the inverse ratio $\frac{24}{25}$.

Every transposition from one tonic to another carries with it the necessity of raising certain of the notes to their sharps, or lowering some others to their flats. That which has been explained for one example holds good for all cases. The tonic can be changed from *c* to *g*, to *e*, to *f*, &c.—that is to say, to each note of the scale. By this operation a quantity of new notes is obtained, and experiment shows that every note of the scale ought to be able to be raised to its sharp. To return to the example of the pianoforte, it is seen that it is necessary to add to the seven white keys of an octave seven black keys, and not five, as is done in practice; as raising to a sharp means rising through the interval $\frac{25}{24}$, and this interval does not exist in the simple musical scale.

This idea may be better explained by an example. Between *e* and *f* there is an interval of a major semitone, $\frac{16}{15}$. If *e* then be raised to its sharp, a note is found by rising through the smaller interval $\frac{25}{24}$, which is near *f*, but lower. *e* sharp, then, does not coincide with *f*, as pianoforte-players are prone to believe.

But there is no need for music to stop at this first transposition. When it is once admitted that the tonic can be changed, for example, from *c* to *g*, it can be then changed from *c* to *c* sharp. The same considerations, therefore, must be made for the superadded seven black keys that have already been made for the white keys. If, then, the tonic be changed successively to each of the sharps, in order to keep the intervals the same it is necessary to raise some of the sharps a semitone, or through another interval of $\frac{25}{24}$. Double sharps are thus obtained, which being composed of two minor semitones, are not exactly equivalent to a whole tone, whether major or minor. In fact, to take a single example, the double sharp of *c* is obtained by multiplying its number of vibrations per second by $\frac{25}{24}$ twice over—that is, by $\frac{625}{576}$. This fraction, then, represents the interval between *c* and *c* double sharp, whilst the interval between *c* and *d* is represented by the considerably greater ratio $\frac{9}{8}$. These two notes, then, are not identical with each other.

The conclusion is thus arrived at, that to take into account all possible transpositions of this kind, it would be necessary to have the seven original notes—seven notes for the sharps, and seven notes for the double sharps.

15. Another class of transpositions carries with it the necessity of lowering by a semitone one or other of the notes of the scale by multiplying by $\frac{24}{25}$, which is called lowering a note to its flat. The same considerations which have been made for the sharps hold good also for the flats.

Reasoning in the same way, the conclusion is arrived at, that seven new notes occur for the flats, and seven others for the double flats. It may be added as a general proposition, that these new notes do not coincide with those already mentioned for the sharps. In executive music, and especially for the pianoforte, it is generally admitted that the sharp of a note is equivalent to the flat of the successive note, that, for example, *c* sharp is equivalent to *d* flat; but this is not strictly accurate. In fact, taking *c* at 1, *c* sharp is expressed by $\frac{25}{24}$. But *d* is $\frac{9}{8}$, whence *d* flat would be $\frac{9}{8}$ multiplied by $\frac{24}{25}$, which gives $\frac{27}{25}$, a value different from and greater than the first. *c* sharp is therefore somewhat lower than *d* flat. Similar considerations can be made for all the other notes at whole intervals. As to the semitones of the scale, the considerations remain the same. If the interval *e* to *f* be taken, for example, which is equivalent to a major semitone, and therefore is represented by $\frac{16}{15}$, as sharps and flats correspond respectively to the intervals $\frac{25}{24}$ and $\frac{24}{25}$, it follows that *e* sharp does not coincide either with *f* flat or *f*, and that therefore four distinct notes must be distinguished—*e*, *f* flat, *e* sharp, and *f*. Indeed, in composition a distinction is made between these four notes, and a composer may not confound them one with another.

It follows that the pianoforte, in order to take into strict account all these exigencies, ought for each octave to have one set of seven keys for the original notes of the scale, and also four other sets, each of seven keys, for the sharps, double sharps, flats, and double flats—that is to say, thirty-five keys in all to each octave. It is true that some of these many notes sensibly coincide with each other, so that even a somewhat smaller number of notes would satisfy scientific exigencies; but it is none the less true that music, especially instrumental music, cannot follow out such great complications.

16. As music, then, has developed in respect to all possible transpositions, many attempts have arisen to diminish the excessive number of notes, and to render practical execution more easy. These attempts are all founded on the principle of abandoning strictly mathematical ratios, and of being content, on the other hand, with approximately correct notes, so long as the error is not too perceptible to the ear, and of considering as the same notes differing but little from each other. The fruit of these manifold attempts, which arose particularly towards the end of the seventeenth and beginning of the eighteenth centuries, is the *temperate scale,* which reached its full development at the middle of the last century, especially by means of the works of *Sebastian Bach,* who dedicated to it forty-eight of his most inspired preludes and fugues. It starts with the principle of making no distinction between the major and minor tone, of confounding the major semitone with the minor semitone, and of considering the sharp of a note as equal to the flat of the succeeding note, so that all the notes of an octave are reduced to twelve only, which are considered equidistant from each other; and it is on this principle that our pianofortes, organs, &c., are constructed, where all the notes comprised in an octave are provided by seven white keys and five black ones.

The temperate scale has become generally accepted; it has so come into daily use that, for the most part, our modern executant musicians no longer know that it is an incorrect scale, born of transition in order to avoid the practical difficulties of musical execution. The great progress made in instrumental music is due to this scale, and, above all, the ever-increasing importance of the pianoforte in social life is to be attributed to it.

But, no doubt, it does not represent all that can be done in this respect. It would certainly be very desirable to return to the exact scale, with a few difficulties smoothed over to meet the requirements of practice; for it cannot be denied that the temperate scale has destroyed many delicacies, and has given to music, founded on simple and exact laws, a character of almost coarse approximation. But before continuing this argument, I will give, as an example, the values of the different scales, so as to make the measure of their differences more striking.

Supposing the fundamental note makes 240 vibrations in a second of time, and calling it *c*, our major scale is represented by the following figures:—

c	*d*	*e*	*f*	*g*	*a*	*b*	*c*
240,	270,	300,	320,	360,	400,	450,	480.

The minor scale by—

240, 270, 288, 320, 360, 384, 432, 480.

The Pythagorean scale, comparable with our major scale—

240, 270, $303\frac{3}{4}$, 320, 360, 405, $455\frac{5}{8}$, 480.

Lastly, the temperate major scale has—

240, $269\frac{2}{5}$, $302\frac{2}{5}$, $320\frac{2}{5}$, $359\frac{3}{5}$, $403\frac{3}{5}$, 453, 480.

If the temperate scale be compared with the mathematical scale, it is seen that with the exception of the fundamental note and the octave, none of the other notes coincide exactly. In the temperate scale all the notes are somewhat modified to a greater or less degree.

Taking, for example, the third, this gives in our example 300 vibrations per second for the exact scale, and $302\frac{2}{3}$ for the temperate scale. Therefore there is a difference in this case of $2\frac{2}{3}$ vibrations per second. It may be said that this difference is small; however, when it is considered that it is equal to about $\frac{2}{3}$ of that furnished by the Pythagorean scale, in which the third is represented by $303\frac{3}{4}$, it must be admitted that it cannot be neglected. It has been seen that in Greek music there was no development of harmony, especially because the third and sixth were dissonant. It must be concluded that our harmony founded on the temperate scale is also very defective.

Another argument must be put forward. The difference in our example between the major and minor third is 12 vibrations per second—the first being 300, and the second 288 vibrations per second. But if 12 vibrations per second in this most delicate and sensitive note are enough to change the character of the fundamental chord of the scale, and of the whole piece of music founded on it, it must be allowed that $2\frac{2}{3}$ vibrations per second cannot be quite immaterial, and must therefore produce a sensible discord.

Lastly, it is known that whenever a chord is not in perfect tune, it gives rise to beats. On the pianoforte these are not very perceptible, but on instruments with full, loud, and sustained notes, such as the organ, they may be recognised in a most unpleasant degree, especially when they are frequent. In the example chosen, they would only be $2\frac{2}{5}$ in a second, which becomes sufficiently unpleasant, although there have been here produced low notes of 200 and 300 vibrations per second. For the high notes the beats are much more frequent. Applying the example to the next higher octave, the number of vibrations per second of the two notes, and with this the number of beats per second, are doubled, which must produce a most unpleasant effect.

Even the resultant notes are considerably altered, and instead of reinforcing existing notes, and entering into the general harmony of the chord, they appear discordant—not indeed loud enough to produce true dissonance, but sufficiently so to disturb the serene quiet and the transparency of a chord.

It follows that music founded on the temperate scale must be considered as imperfect music, and far below our musical sensibility and aspirations. That it is endured, and even thought beautiful, only shows that our ears have been systematically falsified from infancy.*

* Cornue has lately made some most ingenious experiments, in which he measured directly the number of vibrations per second of the notes produced by good singers and violin-players, whilst they executed a pure melody with the greatest possible care. He found that they made use neither of the exact nor of the temperate scale, but of a scale differing but little from the Pythagorean; from which he concludes that the

17. Professor *Helmholtz* has had an harmonicon constructed, on which he can play at will in the exact or temperate scale, on purpose to see if there really is an appreciable difference between them. As soon as the ear becomes a little practised, the difference becomes most striking. In the exact scale the consonant chords become much sweeter, clearer, and more transparent, the dissonant chords stronger and rougher; whilst in the temperate scale all these things are mixed together in one uniform tint without any distinct character. The resultant notes have greater importance in the former, and in general the music acquires a more decided, open, robust, and sweet character. Fact, therefore, demonstrates that the results of theory are not mere speculations or pedantic exaggerations, but that they have a true and real value, such as ought to be accepted even in practice.

The wish may then be expressed that there may be a new and fruitful era at hand for music, in which we shall abandon the temperate scale and return to the exact scale, and in which a more satisfactory solution of the great

Pythagorean scale ought still to be looked upon as the scale of melody, whilst our modern scale must be considered as the scale of harmony.

In truth, this distinction, even if it exist, is of no great practical importance, since pure melody without harmony does not exist at the present day, and would be no longer enjoyed. And it is enough for a song to be accompanied by the most simple harmony, to oblige the singer to adopt the scale of harmony, if he would avoid discord. The fact, however, is very interesting in itself, and merits careful examination. It demonstrates a certain tendency in us to select the Pythagorean scale in melody, and gives a very natural basis to the melodious music of the Greeks.

difficulties of musical execution will be found than that furnished by the temperate scale, which, simple though it may be, is too rude.

But all the stringed instruments, which are the very soul of the orchestra, and the human voice, which will always be the most satisfactory and most mellow musical sound, have their notes perfectly free, and can therefore be shifted at the will of the artist. The return to the exact scale does not present any serious difficulty to them. The same may be said with respect to the wind instruments, which are still very imperfect, notwithstanding the great progress already made, but in which the player can, by changing his lip, somewhat raise or lower the note. A flute or trumpet player can therefore play in the exact scale, just as he already plays in the temperate scale; and the same considerations hold good for the greater part of the wind instruments. It does not therefore appear impossible, or even really difficult, for the full orchestra and chorus to perform a piece of music in the exact scale.

Greater difficulties are met with in the case of instruments with fixed notes, such as the pianoforte and the organ. The pianoforte is, indeed, so imperfect an instrument, that notwithstanding the great reputation which it enjoys, it cannot be given any important place in executive music properly so called. In fact there is no pianoforte in the orchestra, and it is thus confined to the drawing-room and the concert-room. The great defect of the pianoforte is that the notes die away rapidly, whatever may be the skill of the player. Beats and resultant notes are therefore perceived with difficulty. As a consequence, even discord becomes less perceptible, and this is the reason why the sound of an instrument that does not keep in tune from one day to another is tolerated. The pianoforte is, truly, the instrument of the temperate scale; it has been developed, has lived, and probably will decay with it. Its defects have had an observable influence on the music written for it. Sustained melody has been more and more obscured; for it have been substituted infinite and complicated musical figures, scales, cadences, shakes, &c., calculated rather to call up the pride of a brilliant executant than the musical sentiment of the hearers. For the few simple lines of great musical works, were substituted infinite arabesques of a new order of the grotesque.

Reforms of this nature may appear superfluous in the case of an instrument which does not keep in tune. But this is not the case with the organ, which has almost lost its reputation, together with the church in which it is principally used; but, musically speaking, it will always be an instrument of great value. In it the beats and resultant notes are strongly pronounced, and ought therefore to induce us to undertake the important reform of the musical scale. But it is evident that if it be desired to provide the organ with all the notes necessary, it would lead to very great complication; but it appears, according to a proposition of

Helmholtz's, that by starting from somewhat different considerations, it is possible to provide for everything in a very satisfactory manner, with twenty-four notes per octave. This is double the number of keys which we have at present; but when the great ability of our pianoforte-players with twelve keys per octave is taken into consideration, it may well be believed that even twenty-four keys well arranged would not offer insurmountable difficulties of execution; and even if musical complications and arabesques had to be abandoned, true and serious music would only be the gainer.

I will therefore end this chapter by expressing the hope that the temperate scale will eventually be abandoned. It has had its day, and has no longer any real *raison d'être*. Man is capable of a much finer class of music than that performed at the present day. I say this without considering the different schools which at present divide musical Europe, since these considerations hold good for all. But those who consider that the musical province of Italy is to cultivate and develop melody, ought to be the first to try for and to favour such a reform. Singing would gain enormously by it, and a melodious form of music accompanied by simple quiet chords—much more, music formed by several voices—would be enormously increased in value by means of such a reform. The ancient Italian music, the choral music of *Palestrina* and *Basili*, acquires a totally different colouring, and becomes much more intelligible, when it is performed in the exact scale.

This would be a great reform, which could not be effected in a short time; but once made, it would of itself constitute a great progress. If some musical instruments would in part require more or less considerable modification in order to adapt them to these new exigencies, the quartet and choral music can be at once taught and performed in the exact scale.

CHAPTER VIII.

1. QUALITY OR *TIMBRE* OF MUSICAL SOUNDS—2. FORMS ASSUMED BY THE VIBRATIONS, OPTICAL METHOD—3. ANOTHER OPTICAL METHOD—4. PHONAUTOGRAPHIC METHOD—5. LAWS OF HARMONICS—6. QUALITY OR *TIMBRE* OF STRINGS AND OF INSTRUMENTS—7. GENERAL LAWS OF CHORDS—8. NOISES ACCOMPANYING MUSICAL SOUNDS—9. QUALITY OR *TIMBRE* OF VOCAL MUSICAL SOUNDS.

1. THE third characteristic difference of musical sounds is their *quality* or *timbre*. Suppose that the same note is sung by different human voices, and played on the pianoforte, violin, flute, &c., it does not require a delicate musical ear to recognise that these notes, although of the same loudness and pitch, are nevertheless different from each other. Our ear goes even farther in this direction, and not only distinguishes between violin and flute, but even between one violin and another by a different maker. The difference is very marked, and makes itself felt in a most remarkable manner in the price of the instrument. Thus, for example, whilst an ordinary violin costs a few pounds, many hundreds are paid for a good *Stradivarius* or *N. Amati*. The same may be said of all musical instruments, although the difference of price is not so great for most of them, as the modern manufacturers are in a posi-

tion to furnish them in any desired number; whilst violins increase in excellence and value with their age.

The difference of *timbre* is therefore very important, and very characteristic. In the human voice, which constitutes the most agreeable and richest monotone musical instrument, the variety is immense. There are scarcely any two individuals who have exactly the same *timbre* of voice. *Timbre* and inflection are the safest means we have of recognising a person.

But the loudness of a note depends on the width, height, and length of the oscillations producing it. It may then be asked, in what two oscillations, of the same width and length, can differ so as to produce so marked a difference as that of *timbre*.

There are two methods of procedure possible in the study of different forms of oscillation, and of the causes that influence *timbre*. The curve of the oscillations may be traced graphically, and the differences between them may be examined thus, or the sounds produced by different instruments may be analysed in order to see if, besides the principal note that is heard, there are not other concomitant sounds or noises which alter the *timbre* of the simple note, and impress a special character on it. The question will be studied in this treatise by both methods, and they will be illustrated by the most important examples in each. As to the form of vibrations, it will be shown that account must be taken not only of the width and length of the oscillations, but also of the special form of the curve which represents them. Thus, for example, the curves 1, 2, 3, in fig. 30, have all three the same width *ab*, and the same length AB; but the form is different for each one of them, and it is precisely on this special form that that which is called *timbre* depends. It will now be explained how such curves may be made visible.

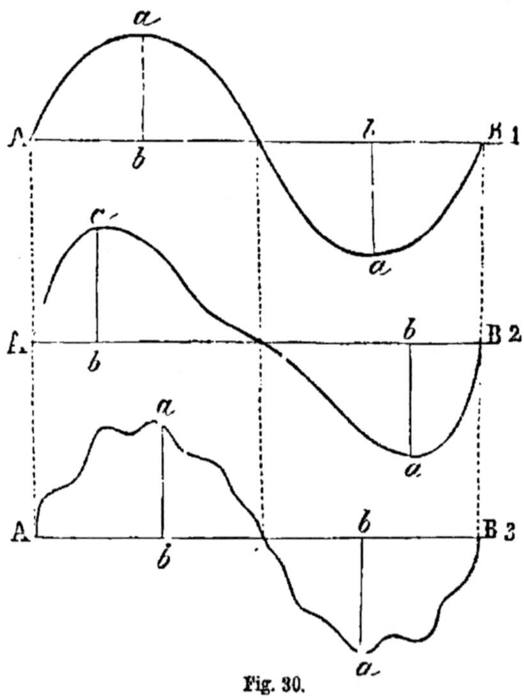

Fig. 30.

2. Of all sonorous bodies the tuning-fork gives the simplest vibrations—vibrations comparable with the oscillations of the pendulum, and which have been called simple vibrations in the first chapter. They have the form of the curve 1 (fig. 30), if they be traced on paper by the graphic method, described in the first chapter.

But they may also be made visible in the following way: A somewhat large tuning-fork F has a small mirror attached near the extremity of one of its branches, and a counterpoise to the other [fig. 31]. A ray of solar

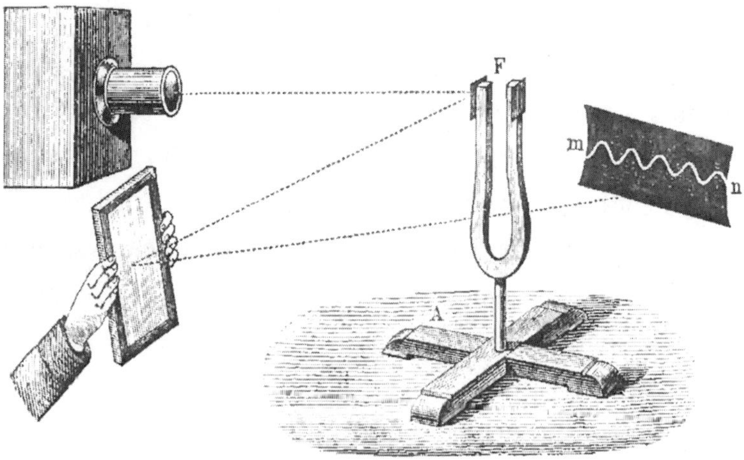

Fig. 31.

light introduced into the room is made to fall on the mirror of the tuning-fork, and is reflected thence on to a concave mirror, and thence again is reflected on to a diaphragm of translucent paper. An image of the hole in the window shutter is thus obtained on the diaphragm under the form of a luminous spot. This spot remains at rest as long as the tuning-fork is at rest, but when the latter vibrates, its mirror takes part in the vibration, and there appears a vertical luminous line instead of the spot on the diaphragm. This line is caused because our eyes are not able to follow the rapid movements of the luminous spot, which occupies a new position at every instant;

but if the concave mirror be rapidly moved by hand, so that it turns round a vertical axis, the different luminous spots, which correspond to different points of time, strike different parts of the diaphragm, and a beautiful curve *mn* is thus formed, which represents the form of the vibrations. In it the width evidently depends on the greater or less degree of energy with which the tuning-fork vibrates; the length depends on the velocity of rotation of the concave mirror, and therefore can be varied at will. But if the mirror be turned with a suitable velocity, neither too fast nor too slow, a most beautiful sinuous curve is obtained, which exactly represents the form of the simple vibrations.

This beautiful optical method of showing the vibrations of tuning-forks, invented by *Lissajous*, is very fertile, and allows a great number of experiments to be made. It is interesting to study what happens when two vibrations are combined together in different ways, when somewhat complex compound movements are the result. One example out of many may be given here, especially as it affords an admirable illustration of the theory of beats (Chapter v.) Fig. 32 shows the arrangement best suited for the present purpose. From the window, or from a closed box L, a pencil of rays of solar or artificial light is caused to enter the room, and having been suitably concentrated by the lens I, falls upon the mirror of a tuning-fork T′, thence by reflection on to that of a second tuning-fork T, and thence, finally, on a diaphragm of paper, where the image of a luminous spot is formed. The tuning-forks are both equal, and give the same note. If the tuning-fork T be now rubbed with a violin bow, it vibrates and changes the luminous spot on the diaphragm into a long vertical line; but if the other tuning-fork T′ be also rubbed, the vertical line becomes longer or shorter, according as the vibratory movements of the two tuning-

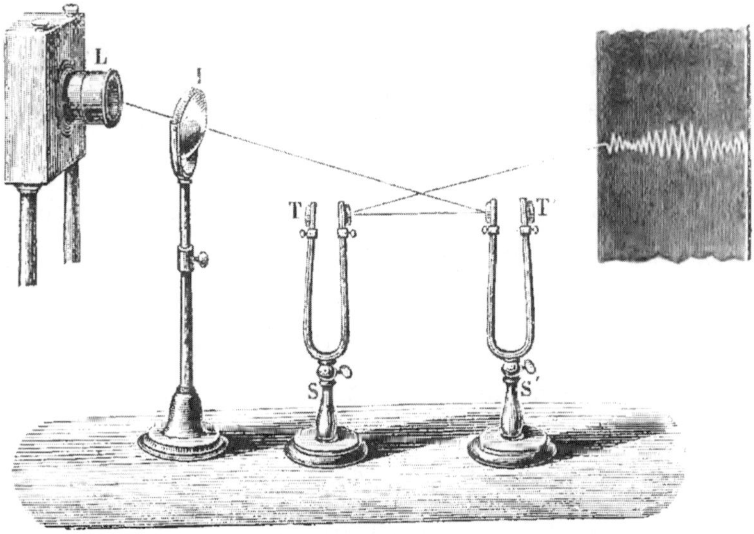

Fig. 32.

forks are made in the same or in reverse directions at the same instant of time, and therefore reinforce or enfeeble each other's effect.

This being so, if a small coin be attached by means of a little wax to the tuning-fork T, it will be retarded in its vibrations, and will thus give with the other T′ very marked beats. The vertical line will then be of variable length —sometimes long and sometimes short, and one of these changes to each beat. The reason is simple. To each beat there corresponds one reinforcement and one enfeebling of the sound, and therefore there is one moment at which the movements of the two tuning-forks are added together, and another at which they enfeeble each other's effect. This vertical line can easily be converted into an undulating line by rapidly moving the tuning-fork T. Fig. 33

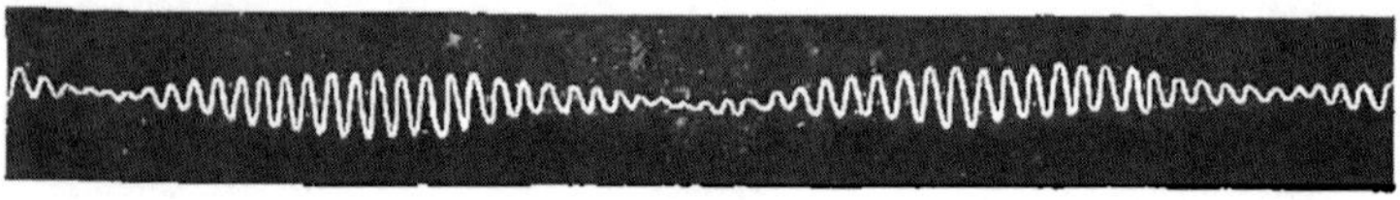

Fig. 33.

is thus obtained, where each reinforcement and enfeeblement are clearly indicated, as also is the whole beautiful form of the phenomenon.

3. It may also be shown that the vibrations of a string are much more complicated than those of a simple tuning-fork. Fig. 34 shows the arrangement necessary for this purpose. A mirror S is so fixed to the window F as to be capable of being turned in all directions; this receives a pencil of solar rays, and sends it into the room through the slit S′. This illuminates the string (or better, a part of the string) of a sonometer A. The image of the string is magnified and projected on a distant screen (not shown in the figure) by means of the lens L.

But if the string be caused to vibrate, the image becomes larger and fainter, because the eye is not able to follow the string in its rapid movement.

In order to see the image of the string clearly at any

particular instant, it is necessary to illuminate it only momentarily, whilst the observers remain in darkness. This can be done, for example, by the electric spark, which has an extremely short duration. But the illumination thus obtained is feeble, and the phenomenon cannot be observed at a little distance off. The slit S′, through

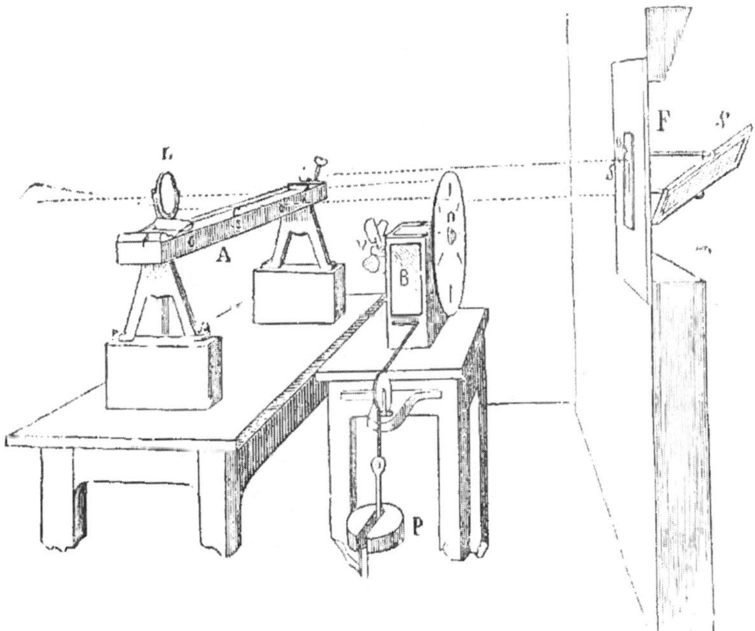

Fig. 34.

which the pencil of solar rays comes which illuminates the string, can be closed and opened again for only a very short time. By this means a very brilliant illumination of the vibrating string is obtained for an instant, and the state of the string at that given instant can thus be made visible. But even this method has the fault that the phenomenon lasts for an exceedingly short time, so that it is difficult to observe it in all its minute details.

This method, however, may be improved by being arranged so as to give an illumination of the string at very short intervals each time that it returns to the same position. An intermittent series of illuminations is thus obtained, and they succeed each other so rapidly that the illumination appears constant, and causes the string to appear as if fixed in the given position. The point, then, is to discover some means of illuminating the string each time that it reaches one and the same position.

For this purpose use may be made of a disc of card-board D (fig. 34), which carries a certain number of narrow slits (eight in all) disposed at equal distances round the circumference of a circle. It can be rapidly turned by means of an excellent rotatory apparatus B, set in motion by the weight P, and regulated by the fly V—an apparatus which allows a uniform motion to be given to the disc, and also allows its velocity to be varied at will. This latter result is easily obtained by increasing more or less the weight P, and modifying the form of the fly; after a few trials it is easy to find the required velocity.

The apparatus then operates as follows: The disc being placed before the slit through which the solar rays enter, intercepts them completely; but every time that one of the slits in the disc comes before the slit in the shutter, the rays pass and illuminate the string. If, then, the velocity of the disc be so chosen that in the time that it takes for the second, third, &c., slit in the disc to come before the slit in the shutter, the string makes a complete movement, and returns to its first position, the string will be illuminated intermittently at equal intervals of time, always when it is in the same position. The string ought to appear fixed, and present the form which it has at the given moment and in the given position. The figures obtained are very clear and complicated, and can easily be drawn, because the phenomenon remains as it were fixed for as long a time as may be wished. But it changes its form according to the way in which the string is made to vibrate. If it be plucked at a third, at a fourth of its length, or at a seventh or eighth, if it be rubbed with a bow at one point or another, sensibly different figures are obtained.

Fig. 35 shows, as an example, the form observed when

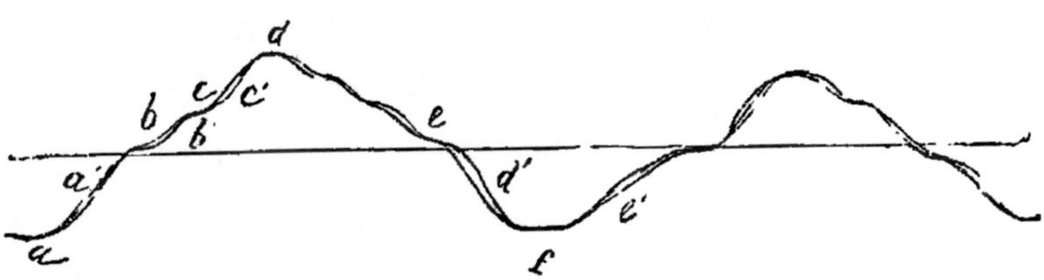

Fig. 35.

the string is plucked at one-seventh of its length. The form is complicated, which is the interesting circumstance. The image is not equally clear and sharp at all its points. At the points *a*, *b*, *c*, *d*, there is a thin black line; at the intermediate points *a'*, *b'*, *c'*, *d'*, the image is enlarged and fainter. The different portions of the string at these latter points undergo very rapid vibrations, which the disc, on account of its too slow rate of rotation, does not succeed in analysing. These portions, then, behave as in the ordinary case of a string illuminated by continuous light, which does not show its form, but only the limits between which it vibrates.

4. An apparatus of much use in many acoustic researches, and especially in the present question, is *Scott's Phonautograph* (fig. 36). A large sounding-board in the form of a paraboloid, open at its large end, and closed at its narrowest part by a very thin animal membrane M, which is stretched more or less by means of three screws *v* (of which only one is shown in the figure). A piece of elder pith *a* cut into a right angle is attached to the membrane, and carries at its extremity a very light and flexible point *p*.

A note produced opposite the paraboloid A is reinforced by it, the membrane M vibrates, the piece *a* takes part in these vibrations leverwise, and the point *p* vibrates strongly in a direction perpendicular to its own length. The vibrations are further made visible by means of the graphic method. The point *p* touches the surface of the revolving cylinder C, and the screw V serves to regulate this contact. The cylinder is covered by a sheet of very smooth paper smoked in a petroleum flame, and a movement of rotation is imparted to the cylinder by means of the handle M, or better still, by means of a clockwork movement arranged to produce uniform rotation, driven by the weight P. The axis of the cylinder C further has a screw cut on it, so that the traces taken by different turns are not superposed.

The phonautograph is a very useful instrument, which

Fig. 36.

may be used for many and various researches. The vibrations of a note are traced by it with great regularity. If two organ-pipes differing slightly from each other be taken and beats be produced, they will be traced with great regularity on the revolving cylinder. Very beautiful curves are thus obtained, similar to those obtained by the optical method [fig. 33].

But this instrument serves not only to demonstrate the vibrations, but may also serve most usefully to make known the form of the special corresponding curve.

In this respect, however, the instrument is not altogether to be relied upon; it may be that it does not register all the partial notes which enter into the formation of the compound note, and it may also be the case that it adds something on its own account.*

But notwithstanding these small defects, it shows admirably that different and very characteristic curves correspond to sounds of different *timbre.* The *modus operandi* is the same in every case. All that is necessary is to produce the sound to be examined before the mouth of the instrument with a sufficient degree of energy, and the instrument then of itself traces the required curve.

Fig. 37 represents some of the most important cases in this respect. Each horizontal line contains two somewhat different curves, which however belong to the same sound, and which are obtained according to the greater or less

* The effect is more certain, and the curves obtained are more beautiful and clearer, when the pith lever is reversed and only attached by one end to the middle of the membrane, and the rectangular lever provided with a joint so that it can move freely. The curves lately obtained thus are much more beautiful and characteristic than those shown in fig. 37.

degree of energy and clearness with which the sound is produced. Generally distinct musical sounds give more complicated and more characteristic curves, than faint sounds.

The first five lines contain the curves obtained by the

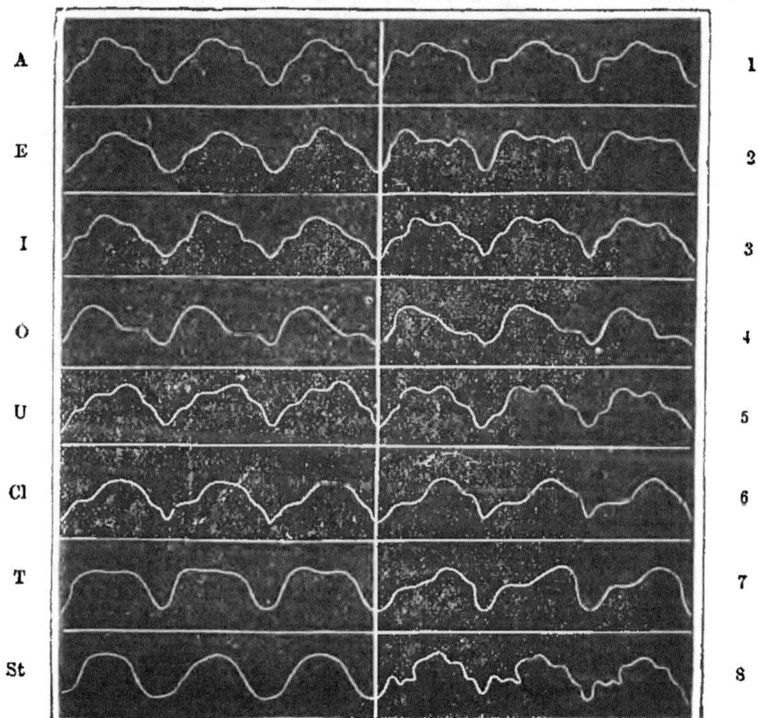

Fig. 37.

vibrations produced by the strong voice of a baritone singing the note *g*, and pronouncing more or less clearly the vowels A, E, I, O, U. The sixth and seventh lines contain the curves obtained from the same note sounded on the clarionet and trumpet. The last contains by way of complement the curve obtained by *Quincke*, by another method, for a vibrating string—the first half when the string was rubbed at one-third, the second when it was rubbed at one-twentieth of its length.

5. All these curves, in their great variety, are certainly interesting, and give rise to another question: In what relation do these complex vibrations stand to the simple vibrations found in the case of the tuning-fork? It may be easily demonstrated that complex vibrations may be considered as the sum of 2, 3, or more simple vibrations. The proposition thus stated is too general for the purposes of this treatise, and must be restricted to the simplest case before us.

As an example, suppose there to be given three vibrations, so chosen that their lengths are inversely as 1 : 2 : 3 [fig. 38]. If it be admitted that these three vibrations are executed simultaneously by the same body, it is fairly easy to determine the curve representing the resultant motion.

For this purpose all that is needed is to draw the vertical lines ab, $a'b'$, $a''b''$, and to set off on these the values for each curve and add them together. The curve 4 is thus drawn, in which each vertical line is equal to the algebraic sum of the corresponding vertical lines of the first three curves. This curve thus produced is the curve required.

In this way the curves of fig. 30 have a clearly determinate meaning. Curve 1 is simple; the second is the result of two sets of vibrations whose lengths are in the proportion of 2 : 1; the third is formed by vibrations whose lengths are as 8 : 1.

It is seen by these examples that a complex curve may

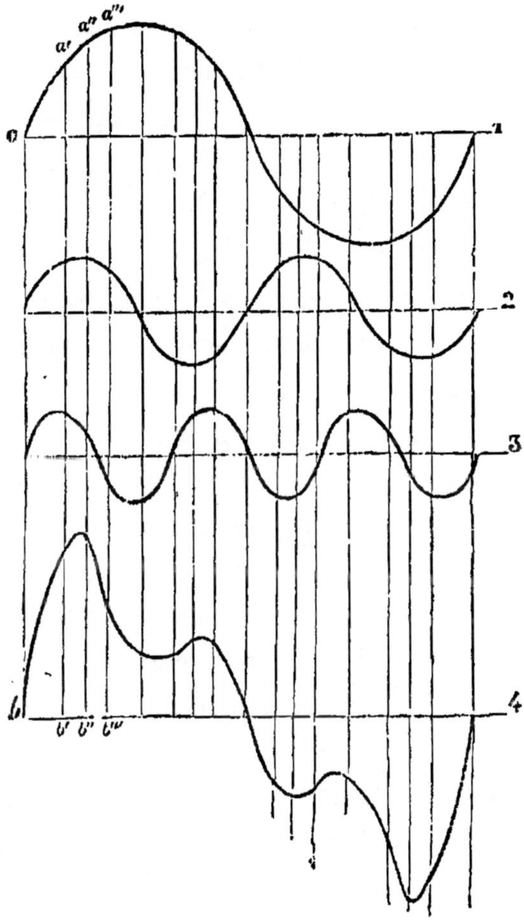

Fig. 38.

be considered as the resultant of certain simple curves, and that the compound curve differs according to the form and number of the simple curves composing it. As a general proposition, it is the more complex, as the number of the curves that compose it is greater and their form more complex.

As simple curves combined together give a complex curve, it may be asked whether every complex curve can be decomposed into simple curves. Proposed in these terms the problem is very general, and can only be solved by mathematical calculation. It will not, therefore be possible to enter on it here; but the great importance of the subject makes it necessary to give, at all events, the result arrived at. Calculation shows that such problems can always be solved.

However complicated the form of a periodic curve may be, it can always be decomposed into a greater or less number of simple curves, if they be so chosen that the relative numbers of the vibrations they represent are in the simple proportion of the progressive numbers 1, 2, 3, 4, 5, &c.

This signifies that a complex curve, representing, for example, the vibrations of a string, can always be decomposed into a curve representing a simple vibration of the same number per second; and, further, into one representing a vibration of double that number, and others representing vibrations of a number triple, quadruple, quintuple, &c., per second. But as vibrations whose numbers per second are as 1 : 2 : 3 : 4 : 5, &c., form the notes in that which has been called the harmonic series, the result of mathematical investigation may be acoustically expressed in the following manner: *Every musical sound whose vibrations have a complex form, as those of a string, can be decomposed into a series of simple notes all belonging to the harmonic series.* With this theorem in hand, we ought to be able to discover in compound musical sounds all the individual simple notes which compose them, and we have thus initiated a second experimental method of studying the *timbre* of musical sounds.

6. Experience shows that the notes of a string are not always simple, but are accompanied by notes of the harmonic series; if a sonometer be taken, for example, and the string be caused to sound so that it gives the fundamental note. The reader already knows that the harmonics are obtained by dividing the string into 2, 3, 4, &c., parts (see Chapter i.), and that the fundamental note being equal to 1, the harmonics are represented by the progressive numbers 2, 3, 4, &c.

Seebeck's siren (fig. 29) also serves admirably for producing the harmonics. If there be placed on the axis of rotation a disc which contains the following concentric series of holes:—

8, 16, 24, 32, 40, 48, 56, 64,

which are in the ratios of—

1 : 2 : 3 : 4 : 5 : 6 : 7 : 8,

the harmonics of the fundamental note are produced in absolutely correct proportions. These notes must not be confounded with those of the musical scale. They are, especially the first, very distant from each other.

In fact, from the fundamental note 1 we pass to its octave 2, thence to the fifth of its octave 3, and thence to the second octave above 4; whilst in the musical scale the successive notes are considerably closer together.

This being understood, it is not difficult to demonstrate that in the case of a vibrating string the fundamental note is accompanied by its harmonics. With a little attention, and without recourse to special experiments, the presence of the third harmonic may be perceived by the ear alone. The latter becomes especially perceptible when the sound of the string has grown faint, because the fundamental note dies away more rapidly than the third harmonic, and therefore makes it more prominent; also the fifth harmonic is easily perceptible. The second and fourth harmonics are less quickly perceived, because they represent the first and second octaves of the fundamental note, and are easily confounded with it.

The same fact is met with in the strings of a pianoforte. Sounding a somewhat low note—a *c*, for example—the octave of the next, *g*, is easily perceived, which is its third harmonic, and the *e* of the next octave, which is its fifth harmonic. The other harmonics can also be heard, but with greater difficulty. The seventh harmonic is wanting, because pianofortes are generally so constructed that the hammer strikes the string almost exactly at the point which corresponds to a node of the seventh harmonic —that is to say, strikes at a seventh of the length of the string, which prevents the formation of a node at that point.

Harmonics are met with also in other instruments; but if they are difficult to perceive, as often happens, either because they are too much mixed up with the fundamental note, as is the case with the human voice, or because they are too feeble, recourse may be had with great success to *Helmholtz's* resonators (see fig. 22).

It has been seen [Chapter iii.] that these are nothing more than sounding-boards of spherical or cylindro-conical form which are fitted to the ear, and which reinforce, each one, according to its volume, some one particular note. It is enough to be provided with a series of these resonators for the different notes that may be met with, to have a very efficacious means of proving the presence of any particular note, however feeble it may be, in the midst of many others. The researches made on this point demonstrate that musical sounds produced by different instruments have different harmonics, or at least in a different measure.

A note not accompanied by its harmonics may sometimes be sweet, but it is always thin and poor, and therefore but little musical. This is the case with tuning-forks. Even the stopped organ-pipe is almost without harmonics; the result is, that it gives a hollow and by no means agreeable sound, somewhat like the vowel *u*. The harmonics become, therefore, an almost indispensable condition of musical sounds properly so called. When the fundamental note is accompanied by the lower harmonics 2, 3, &c., it acquires a broad, open, soft character. If, on the other hand, it is the higher harmonics that prevail, the sound acquires a shrill or clanging character—as, for example, in the trumpet, &c.

The richest in harmonics are the sounds of the human voice and of strings, and it is for this reason that instruments of this class are, and always will be, the most musical.

7. The *timbre* of musical sounds is produced, then, by the presence, in greater or less number and degree, of the harmonics which accompany the fundamental note. A musical sound is always a compound sound, its vibrations are more or less complicated, and it by itself alone constitutes a true harmony, especially if the seventh harmonic be wanting, which does not form a part of our musical system. It follows that in combining two, three, or more musical sounds in order to form a chord, it is not enough that the fundamental notes should bear simple ratios to each other, but it is also necessary that the harmonics should obey this law. Also the resultant notes, which may be formed by all these notes, must enter into the same system of harmony. We can thus formulate a law for harmony not only vaster and more general, but also, as will be hereafter seen, even more simple.

In fact, suppose that there be given the fundamental note 1; the harmonics will be represented by 2, 3, 4, 5, &c., whence the complication of notes will be expressed by—

1, 2, 3, 4, 5, &c.

Suppose that the octave be also given, which is represented by 2, and with it the harmonics of the doubled numbers—

$$2, 4, 6, 8, \&c.$$

It is seen that, in fact, the octave does not possess a single new note. It only repeats certain of the harmonics of the fundamental note; therefore by combining together the fundamental note and the octave, the only effect produced is the reinforcement of some of the harmonics already existing in the fundamental note. It follows that the fundamental note and octave cannot strictly be considered as two separate musical sounds; their harmony constitutes one single musical sound of somewhat modified *timbre*. And this is what really takes place in instruments that are rich in harmonics—as, for example, the violin.

Adding the fifth, which is represented by $\frac{3}{2}$, to this chord, the harmonics comprised in the fifth itself will be—

$$\tfrac{3}{2}, 3, \tfrac{9}{2}, 6, \&c.$$

Some of these notes, as 3, 6, &c., are comprised in the fundamental note; but $\frac{3}{2}$, $\frac{9}{2}$, &c., are new notes. The chord with the fifth is less perfect than that with the octave; but we can make it more perfect by adding as a reinforcement the octave below the fundamental note, which is expressed by $\frac{1}{2}$, and has for harmonics—

$$\tfrac{1}{2}, 1, \tfrac{3}{2}, 2, \tfrac{5}{2}, 3, \&c.$$

Referring the fifth to this low note, we see that all its harmonics are already comprised in those of the latter; in fact, $\frac{3}{2}$, $\frac{9}{2}$, &c., are the third, ninth, &c., harmonics of the fundamental note $\frac{1}{2}$. In this way the harmony becomes more perfect. This is the reason why the chord of the fundamental note with the fifth and octave sounds rather hollow and poor, and is considerably improved when the lower octave of the fundamental note is added.

A somewhat similar conclusion is arrived at by adding to this same chord the major third, which with its harmonics is expressed by—

$$\frac{5}{4}, \frac{5}{2}, \frac{15}{4}, \text{\&c.}$$

These notes do not exist in the fundamental note, but if the second octave below the fundamental note, which is expressed by $\frac{1}{4}$, be added, they all become harmonics, though distant ones, of this note.

The conclusion to be drawn from this is that it is necessary to add to the perfect chord of fundamental note, major third and octave, the two octaves below, in order to render it really agreeable. This conclusion agrees with that which experience has taught for a great length of time. In fact, in practical music this chord is always written as is shown below at 1, and never as at 2 or 3.

It may appear strange that in the perfect chord the

fundamental note and its octaves should occupy four places, whilst the third and fifth occur only once, and it might appear that in this arrangement there was a want of balance between the different notes.

Certainly this preponderance of the fundamental note would be inexplicable by the laws developed in the preceding chapters, when account was taken only of the simple ratios. The reason becomes evident by the considerations just now made; it is, that in the perfect chord all the notes must be considered as a simple reinforcement of the fundamental note. The perfect chord becomes, in fact, a single musical sound, of very musical quality, and with a very rich and varied *timbre.*

The conclusion is thus arrived at, that chords are so much the more agreeable to the ear as fewer new notes are added to the fundamental note; in the most agreeable chord of all, the perfect chord, not a single new note is added. This conclusion becomes the more evident, the richer the musical sounds at our disposal are in harmonics. It is also easily explained by the conformation of the ear, which finds a chord the more agreeable, the less effort is necessary to understand it.

8. The *timbre* of musical sounds is not only caused by the harmonics which accompany in different degrees the fundamental note, but also by the more or less distinct noises which are caused by the special method by which the sounds are produced. A string rubbed by a bow always allows the sound of something scraping to be

heard; at the embouchure of an organ-pipe the blowing of the air is heard; in the pianoforte the hammer is distinctly heard as it strikes the string, and so on. Generally speaking, as we are accustomed to hear these noises from our earliest infancy, it is these above all that teach us to distinguish one instrument from another, whilst the harmonics are unnoticed, although they may be much louder than the noises spoken of.

In fact, if the harmonics that accompany a note on the violin are always the same, as, with the exception of very slight differences, is really the case, there is no reason in practical life to induce us to go farther into the matter, or to analyse and examine as to the extent to which they may be present. It is for this reason that the harmonics remained so long unobserved, and that even now many practical musicians are unacquainted with them, or look upon them as subjective phenomena.

Our ear does not advance in analysis farther than it ought; it obeys, in this respect, also that which appears to be a fundamental law of nature—that is, it obtains its purpose with the least exertion and the least labour possible. It may be easily demonstrated that the ear does not separate notes to the concomitance of which it has been long accustomed. By taking a series of tuning-forks giving the harmonic series, and setting them in action, in a short time their notes become so mixed together as to appear only one note. If, then, another tuning-fork, which by itself gives a good harmony with the fundamental note—as, for example, $\frac{5}{2}$—but which is not a harmonic of the fundamental note 1, be set vibrating, the presence of this new note almost immediately disturbs the equilibrium of the harmonics; the ear is then induced to analyse what it perceives, and all the notes are distinctly heard. For the same reason it is very difficult to perceive the harmonics of the human voice, however numerous and strongly pronounced they may be. It is necessary for this to have recourse to more minute methods of analysis, and in this respect Helmholtz's resonators are of the greatest use. But at the same time I will describe an instrument founded on the use of resonators, and constructed by the mechanician *König* for the purpose of making the results visible even to a numerous audience.

9. The apparatus (fig. 39) is composed of eight resonators adapted to the harmonic series of the fundamental note *c*. At the back of each one an indiarubber tube puts the orifice in communication with a capsule, closed by an elastic membrane. In front of this, gas enters and burns under the form of a small, very mobile flame. Eight flames, therefore, correspond to the eight resonators. When the air vibrates in one of the resonators, the vibration is communicated to the flame, and its vibrations are observed, as is described in the first chapter, by means of a revolving mirror, which is turned by a handle. In order to know if the sound of a given instrument or of the human voice contains harmonics, and what they

may be, all that is needful is to produce close to the apparatus a note corresponding in pitch to the largest resonator—that is to say, *c*—which represents the fundamental note. Then, if there be harmonics, they will set

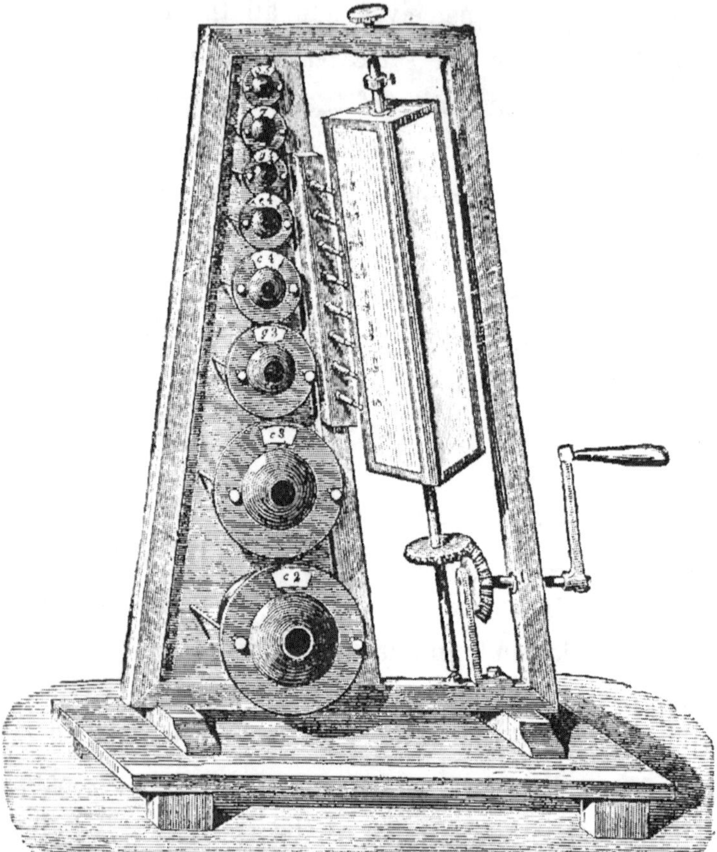

Fig. 39.

the resonators in action, and thence the corresponding flames, and a glance at the revolving mirror is all that is required in order to recognise them immediately.

By means of this most ingenious instrument it may be demonstrated that all musical instruments have harmonics, and it is immediately seen which these harmonics are.

The same may be said of the human voice, which is very rich in these notes. If a *c* be sung near the instrument, many flames will be seen to vibrate. But, following the example of *Helmholtz*, it may be demonstrated that the different vowels pronounced whilst singing a note give different harmonics. In order to show this, sing the fundamental note, and at the same time pronounce successively the different vowels. The harmonics can thus be easily observed, which accompany the fundamental note in different degrees. The following results are obtained in the case we are considering:—

The vowel *U* is composed of the fundamental note very strong, and the third harmonic sufficiently pronounced.

O contains the fundamental note, the second harmonic very strong, and the third and fourth harmonics slightly.

The vowel *A* contains, besides the fundamental note, the second harmonic feeble, the third strong, and the fourth feeble.

E has the fundamental note feeble, the second harmonic rather strong, the third feeble; on the other hand, the fourth is very strong and the fifth feeble.

I has very high harmonics, especially the fifth, strongly marked.

These differences, which are easily observed, arise from

the forms assumed by the mouth, tongue, and lips in the pronunciation of the different vowels. They are not exactly the same, as they depend on the *timbre* of the voice of the person pronouncing them, on the special character of the language in which they are pronounced, and also on the pitch of the note selected as the fundamental note. This last fact may be understood when it is considered that the mouth itself acts as a resonator of variable form and size. The results, therefore, are complicated, and I will only draw attention to them.

But if it be true that the *timbre* of the vowels is constituted in the way briefly indicated above, we ought to be able to reproduce the different vowels by synthesis, by combining the fundamental note with its harmonics in the proper proportions. This work has been actually accomplished by *Helmholtz*, who made use for this purpose of stopped organ-pipes, which gave sensibly simple notes. He arranged them according to the harmonic series, and combining them together in the way indicated above, succeeded in making the fundamental pipe *speak* the different vowels in a clearly pronounced manner. The demonstration is therefore complete, and certainly constitutes one of the great triumphs of science.

CHAPTER IX.

1. DIFFERENCE BETWEEN SCIENCE AND ART—2. ITALIAN AND GERMAN MUSIC—3 AND 4. SEPARATION OF THE TWO SCHOOLS—5. INFLUENCE OF PARIS—6. CONCLUSION.

1. THE laws of *timbre* are the basis of the theory of instrumentation, and also embrace the whole of harmony. Thanks to them, all that has been explained heretofore is reducible to one single principle—that is, *That musical notes must satisfy the laws of harmony, and that this is the more perfect, the more the notes of a chord reinforce the fundamental note.* Thus the idea of tho tonic and the fundamental chord loses its character of only practical utility; it becomes a necessary consequence of this law.

Science has succeeded in taking in from one single point of view this grand and admirable assemblage of facts, which are required in the history and development of music. It is in a position to deduce rigorously the rules of the art of music, and could easily create it anew if it happened to be lost.

But I should not wish these words of mine to raise in the minds of my readers the idea that science can be or desires to be substituted for art. In art there is one thing that escapes all calculation, which science indeed can explain up to a certain point when it has taken a palpable form, but which it can neither predict or modify: this is Poetic Inspiration. As the most profound knowledge of grammar, of syntax and prosody, is not sufficient to make even a mediocre poet, so the most accurate study of the laws of harmony and of instrumentation would not be enough to create a composer. Composition and criticism are two diametrically opposite operations of the human mind: they ought to go hand in hand, and as far as possible with a common agreement, and be complementary one to the other; but the critic will never be a great composer, nor the composer a true critic.

I have endeavoured to pass before my readers in rapid review the most important facts of the history of music, and have especially endeavoured to show how even the most fantastic creations of man may be linked to certain simple laws which science has revealed. These laws were certainly unknown to those great men of genius who have left an imperishable record in their works. They were only guided in their paths by feeling, fancy, and inspiration. Science came afterwards and only explained. And it will always be thus even in the future. The thought, therefore, will never enter into our mind to prophesy what music will be fifty or a hundred years hence, and, artistically speaking, it will be on the ascending or descending branch of the parabola; the more so as the æsthetic principles to which the art successively conforms have no absolute value. But it may be said with certainty that no single thing will ever be accepted which is clearly contrary to the broad principles already established by science. And with this my task would be finished: but I do not wish to leave this interesting subject, or to close this treatise, without touching on some few other questions which have latterly been much agitated, and which belong to the artistic patrimony of modern Europe.

2. Much has been said about the great substantial difference separating the Italian and German music. The former is called simple, intelligible, and melodious; the latter complicated, studied, obscure, and transcendental. And it is sought to find in this one of the characteristic features of difference between the two nations. It is true that in the last and present centuries Italian musicians have cultivated by choice melody and song, and it is also true that in German music the study of harmony and of choral and instrumental scoring has been carried to an admirable degree of perfection; but it is not true that this has always been the case, and it would be a great error to endeavour to find in these facts a distinctive characteristic of the two nations.

In the Middle Ages matters were exactly reversed; the first centuries of polyphonic music were marked in Italy by immense complication. Voices linked together in a most artificial manner, different movements fused together according to complicated and obscure rules, were the characteristics of Italian polyphonic music up to the time of *Palestrina.* The Protestant Reformation produced in Germany simple harmony and simple song, a form of music at once clear, easy, and transparent. No comparison is possible as to simplicity between the first Protestant chants and the Italian music of this same Palestrina, who was, however, the great reformer and simplifier of Italian polyphonic music.

After this epoch the two nations continued, in respect to style, almost on the same road. Italy decidedly took the lead, thanks to her enormous musical activity, and to the considerable number of men of real creative power.

From this moment progress was rapid and continuous. *Viadana* wrote the first melodies, and added as their accompaniment the continuous bass; *Carissimi* and *Scarlatti* may be considered as the inventors of expressive recitative. To this last true musical genius we owe the invention of the *aria,* which with its first and second part and repetition represents in music almost that which the column represents in architecture. In his operatic essays he introduced the *recitativo obligato,* and initiated by this the change from the first Italian style to the second, a change which his great disciples and emulators *Durante, Leo,* and *Greco* thoroughly effected. Thanks to their efforts, music threw off its character of great severity, and its rigid rules of harmony and counterpoint. In their hands, and in those of the bold innovator *Claudio Monteverde*, it, on the contrary, underwent considerable instrumental development, with more broadly and freely distributed melody, followed by accompaniments of greater simplicity and of freer scope. For the austere movement was substituted clear, simple, ingenuous sentiments; plastic beauty, exact time, maintained with grace and fine discrimination in the midst of most beautiful melodies, was the character assumed by music in the seventeenth century, a character which is especially to be recognised in the ecclesiastical music; whilst in opera, notwithstanding all efforts, the form still remained very primitive. This movement continued up to the eighteenth century. Following close on church music, opera developed more and more, and with the history of this movement the names of *Pergolese, Piccini, Sacchini, Jomelli, Cimarosa,* and *Paesiello* remain connected. This creative activity was communicated to Germany, where it took a new form and a surprising development. Men like *Händel, Haydn, Bach, Gluck, Mozart,* gave a wonderful breadth of idea to music; but, with the exception of *Gluck,* they must be considered as the fruitful and genial continuers of the Italian movement, which they carried out in much the same spirit as the Italian composers themselves. To show how little the two differed, we need only compare the "Matrimonio segreto" of *Cimarosa* with *Mozart's* "Nozze di Figaro." One would say that they were two works of the same school, and composed by two brothers in art, of which the first was the most facile, most cheerful, and most elegant; the second the broader, richer, and more profound.

3. The distance between the German and Italian music is most evident in the case of the works of *Gluck* and *Beethoven* on the one hand, and the works of *Rossini* on the other. Whilst in the middle of the last century the two schools did not differ much from each other, and the Italian music then closely resembled the German, the executive part of the art took a different direction in Italy. The last century is the century of grand Italian song. Italy surprised the world by the number of distinguished singers she produced, and by the serious and solid method on which her schools of singing were organised. These singers overran Europe, passing from triumph to triumph, fêted by all, and idolised in an almost incredible manner. But it was precisely the great importance to which the Italian school of singing rose which became the cause of its downfall in real value. The singers began to consider themselves as the thing of greatest importance, and as the basis on which the grandeur of Italian music reposed. For them the composition was the pretext; their principal aim, to shine as much as possible. It then came about that the music being too simple to afford them the means of shining, they substituted for simple melody a more complicated form, interpolating turns and shakes, cadences and ornamentations of every kind, to the manifest detriment of the composer and of musical good taste. The great masters of that time submitted to this state of

things, being powerless to remedy it. Then came *Rossini*, who thought it better to write complicated melodies with scales, cadences, and difficulties of every sort himself, since thus alone could good taste be even partially saved. He acted like certain politicians, who put themselves at the head of a movement in the hope of being thus better able to control it.

The richness and variety of his forms are truly admirable; but it is evident that true musical conception must suffer under these continued shakes and turns. There is only one purpose for which this light and varied style seems fitted, and that is for comic opera; and in this respect Rossini has left an undying model of grace and freshness in the "Barbiere di Siviglia." In his later works, in the style of grand opera, Rossini abandoned this style almost completely. His last opera, "Guglielmo Tell," is entirely without ornamentation, and in some parts—as, for example, in the trio and in the conspiracy in the second act—rises to an incomparable elevation.

But this more chaste and correct style of Rossini's was formed away from Italy, by tendencies and ideas different from those that there held sway. For Italy, the alienation was effected, and could not easily be again undone. Under his more important successors, as *Bellini* and *Donizetti*, music acquired the character of simple song—often deep and feeling, often light, superficial, and cloying.

The impression which the composer of "Norma" has

produced, and still produces by his beautiful and deeply-felt melodies, the interest that Donizetti inspires by the elegance of style displayed in his best works, ought not to make us lose sight of the fact that the superabundance of melody is not suited to the requirements of the modern stage. Save for many very beautiful exceptions, sentimentality took the place of real sentiment; and dramatic expression was to a great extent obscured, and often never sought after. Then came *Verdi,* who felt that this continual melody would at last corrupt all minds. For beautiful melody he substituted movement, which was not yet dramatic feeling, but contained strength and vigour, even though it were sometimes in a rather rugged form. This style of writing was pleasingly in accordance with the national aspirations. Italy at that time was awaking to a new life; she felt the want of movement and strong emotions. Patriotism therefore laid hold of the music of Verdi, made it entirely popular, and used and abused it freely. But musical good taste and the school of singing suffered immensely. Latterly, Verdi has considerably modified his style of writing, and has openly drawn nearer to the German school, or has at all events diminished the great distance which formerly separated our school of music from the German school.

From "Nabucco" and "Ernani" to "Rigoletto" and "Il Ballo in Maschera," and from these to "Aida," the progress in this direction is continuous. These examples, besides being well known, are discussed everywhere with interest and eagerness.

4. Although the rupture came from the Italian side, it was first brought about on the side of Germany. *Gluck* introduced and developed wonderfully the conception of dramatic music, which proposes as its object to adapt the music better to the words, and to create a musical work of art capable of producing on the hearers the same sensations that the text which accompanies it produces. In this respect music is an inexhaustible mine of truly artistic effects. It is superior in many points to poetry—sometimes in the expression of the terrible, and sometimes in the expression of the really gentle emotions. To prove this, it is enough to recall in modern works the love scene between Faust and Marguerite described musically by *Gounod*, to conclude that the grand poetry of Goethe has not only not suffered here, but that the effect is somewhat modified and idealised rather than diminished. We need only recall again the duet between Raoul and Valentina, in "Gli Ugonotti," in which all emotions from patriotism to love, and from love to terror, are described with vividness and incomparable feeling, which, in spite of some exaggerations, strike us profoundly; lastly, the terrible scene in *Weber's* "Der Freischütz," where terror is carried to the highest degree of musical expression. Music, which in many respects remains inferior to poetry, shows itself, on the other hand, superior to it in others where dramatic effect and feeling are strongly marked.

A greater separation took place, caused by *Beethoven*, the great and true creator of modern instrumental music. From this time the German school separated more and more from the common road it had trodden in company with the Italian school. *Mendelssohn*, *Schuman*, and lastly *Wagner*, are only a continuous gradation on this path. Music acquired a more and more instrumental character, and free singing became obscured. To use a celebrated phrase, which is perhaps exaggerated, but which sharply depicts the actual state of things, it may be said that in Italian music the orchestra had become a big guitar, only intended to accompany the singing; but it may also be said that in the German music the singers had become walking orchestral instruments. It must, however, be admitted that whilst Italian music has undergone in this century a sensible decline, in Germany it has remained elevated. The study of harmony and grand orchestral movements and deep dramatic feeling and expression, notwithstanding some too realistic exaggerations and some trivialities, have been brought to a high degree of perfection by the intellectual influence of *Richard Wagner*. We owe it to him, that for libretti—almost always insipid, and which served as bare excuses for the musical part of the work—has been substituted a more masculine and independent form of poetry. The closer union of poetry and music, in which both arts advance with regular step without one being smothered by the other, constitutes perhaps the most salient and most beautiful character of his music, which is almost always lofty, most rich, and which transports us to an ideal sphere.

I say this in spite of all the clamour which has been raised on both sides of the Alps against the "music of the future." It is reproached with being too studied and too refined, and with leaning not towards feeling, but calculation and combination.

But we need only listen to it with attention and without prejudice to be convinced of the greatness and number of the beauties which it contains. The prelude to "Lohengrin," the song to the swan, many passages in "Tannhaüser," and other things prove the contrary. This music has had the great and sad privilege of exciting, almost incredibly, passions in its favour and against it; but when these passions have grown calm, I believe that it will be impossible to deny to it the character of a great musical poem whose limits will extend far beyond the national circle for which it was written.

5. Finally, we must take into account a third important agent in musical history—that is, the influence exercised by Paris on the conduct of musical ideas. If we except *opera comique* (which must not be confounded with the Italian *opera buffa*), in which *Grétry, Boieldieu, Hérold, Auber*, and others excelled, it may be said that the French have never been true creators in music. Notwithstanding this, the influence of Paris on the history of the art is great and incontestable. Placed, as it were,

midway between the two musical nations, thanks to the splendours of Parisian life and its mania for amusement, Paris became one of the important centres where many grave musical problems were worked out. It was there that arose the struggle between *Gluck's* severe music and the melodious music of *Piccini.* It was there that the Italian *Cherubini* found a highly honoured post, with his tendency towards German music. It was there that *Meyerbeer,* abandoning his first style, created "Roberto il Diavolo," "Gli Ugonotti," and the "Prophète," which by their grandeur of conception will make his fame immortal. Finally, it is there that the best Italian masters have gone in search of competent criticism, and have modified their style. *Rossini's* "Guglielmo Tell," *Donizetti's* "Favorita" and "Don Sebastian," finally, most of *Verdi's* works, have arisen in this manner. The influence of Paris may be thus defined: that she insists on the creation of a type of music which should contain the good points of the German and Italian schools without their exaggeration. This school is therefore eminently eclectic, and has found the solution of its problems by clinging closely to dramatic music. It thus maintained the Italian melody and song, but limited it to those cases in which it is compatible with dramatic expression. It has adopted the grand choral and orchestral movements of Germany, giving them a suitable importance. Lastly, it tried to obtain an intimate relation between words and music, with the desire, rather expressed than carried out, of subordinating neither to the other.

The character of this school is best recognised in the French composers who have written dramatic operas. *Halévy, Gounod, Auber,* himself in his "Masaniello," have trodden this path. Whatever may usually be thought of eclectic things, the eclecticism of the Paris school has been of real importance. It must be considered as an earnest and partly successful attempt to unite from one common point of view two schools whose tendencies were very different. And from this attempt have arisen noble ideas and grand works of art which will exert a true and great influence even on posterity.

6. As for the future itself, it is not for a musical or scientific critic to wish to foresee its steps. I shall therefore take care not to give an opinion on the subject. That which it was important for us to demonstrate was that music has been developed according to certain rules which depended on unknown laws of nature since discovered, that it cannot be separated from these laws, and that within them there is a field large enough for all the efforts of human fancy.

THE END.